The Resilience Game Plan

The Playbook for Developing Cognitive, Communication, and Mindfulness Life Skills

Facilitator's Guide

for Middle School and High School Student Editions

by
Colleen Carter Ster, A.L.M.
Cheryl James-Ward, Ed.D.

• About the Authors •

Colleen Carter Ster earned her Master of Liberal Arts from Harvard University's Division of Continuing Education in Psychology in 2023 out of concern for the self-harm cases among youth worldwide. Ster created *The Resilience Game Plan: The Playbook for Developing Cognitive, Communication, and Mindfulness Skills* to provide a curriculum for middle schools, high schools, and colleges to help adolescents and emerging adults build resilience by giving them tools to understand how the brain works and help them deal with difficult life situations.

In the mid to late 1990s, Ster served as Executive Vice President for The Electronic Bookshelf (EBS). During her time at EBS, she created curriculum questions for K-12th grade students and developed continuing education credit materials for EBS Reading Power Seminars. Ster conducted training seminars to administrators, library media specialists, and teachers around the United States for several years. In 1998, EBS was acquired by Scholastic, Inc., and Ster became the Director of Marketing Services for Scholastic Reading Counts! in the Learning Ventures Division of Scholastic in New York, New York.

During Ster's years traveling around the United States conducting "Reading Power" training seminars for EBS, she listened to what types of books educators were looking to purchase for their students. Time and again, the answer was to find literature to help students when they were struggling with difficult life scenarios. In 2008, Ster addressed this need by founding a children's publishing business, Reflections Publishing LLC. *ALA Booklist* called the first Reflections Publishing LLC book series "a unique series by children, for children." This special collection by Reflections Publishing LLC is a book series called "Kids Helping Kids Through Books."

As a Girl Scout leader, Ster consulted with her troop members and developed the Reflections Publishing Communication Assessment. Since 2008, this assessment has been a useful tool for K-12 students and their caregivers (parents/guardians), emerging young adults, and adults. The purpose of the assessment is to help individuals understand how their communication skills play a role and affect the way they communicate with others. Ster wants children, tweens, teens, and emerging adults to understand that communication skills are valuable interpersonal tools for them to learn at a young age so they can use these skills during their academic years, when entering into personal relationships, and navigating professional work environments. The Reflections Publishing Communication Assessment and its concepts are incorporated throughout *The Resilience Game Plan* playbook.

Ster is vested in continuing her education to keep *The Resilience Game Plan* an up-to-date and valuable tool for elementary, middle, and high schools and colleges. As a postgraduate student in the University of Oxford's Department for Continuing Education, Ster developed in-person and HyFlex training materials that best support users of *The Resilience Game Plan* intervention program.

With a focus on taking neuroscience, neurobiology, self-harm, and cognitive behavior therapy courses, Ster is determined to try to reduce self-harm cases among youth around the world. Ster wants to get *The Resilience Game Plan* into the hands of every student—providing students their best chance to obtain strong, short- and long-term developmental and well-being outcomes.

Proudly born and raised in Indiana, Ster has called San Diego home for more than 20 years, and is married with three daughters and a son-in-law.

• About the Authors •

Dr. Cheryl James-Ward started her career as a software engineer for NASA Jet Propulsion Laboratory in Pasadena, California working on the Magellan Project which sent a spacecraft to Venus. Because of her love for education, she took a leave from aerospace and pursued her first love, teaching. She never looked back and served as a math teacher, dean of discipline, vice principal, principal, director supervising elementary and middle schools, a tenured professor, a CEO of a charter organization and superintendent of schools.

Dr. James-Ward served as the Chief of Academics and then CEO for e3 Civic High, noted as one of the most innovative schools in the nation. At e3, Dr. Ward worked with her team to create a new way of teaching and learning called Voice and Choice which allowed students to have self-efficacy in their own education. After lunch students would be the architects of their learning by designing how to use their afternoon time. This included opportunities for community college dual enrollment, internships, study time, tutoring, design thinking projects, e-sports, wealth building sessions, and more. Under Dr. James-Ward, e3 Civic High was also a leader in developing mental health support systems, creating wrap-around services for students and families; one-on-one, group and family counseling sessions led by licensed therapists and interns; Saturday parent and student support groups; and a system-wide approach to responding to mental challenges with levels of care and second/third-level responders.

Most recently, Dr. James-Ward was Superintendent of Schools for a High School District. In her tenure, she started site walks with district and site leadership teams to ensure that every child was seen, supported and educated to the highest levels. She initiated community collaborations to further ensure that all students had the support needed. She met with the student leadership teams on various campuses to understand their unique needs and provided opportunities for students from each school to showcase their work through the creation of Talk Around Towns.

From 2007 to 2023, Dr. James-Ward was a tenured professor at San Diego State University (SDSU). From 2013-2018, she dedicated her research to 2030 schools. Dr. James-Ward's research led to her becoming a maverick in Design Thinking and training both districts and schools in the process. This is how she came to e3 and enjoyed working at both the university and e3 for several years. Some of her other accomplishments at the University include establishing the Online Masters in Educational Leadership (with a focus on technology) which after just five years was ranked 11th in the nation by BestColleges.com. She also started the Chinese and American Leadership Symposium bringing educators from across The People's Republic of China to collaborate and innovate with those from San Diego County.

Currently, Dr. James-Ward enjoys the title Professor Emeritus, continues to chair dissertation committees, teach doctoral courses and is committed to making a difference for the most at-promise students by supporting them through self care advocacy and mathematics education.

Dr. Ward is married with two children and resides in San Diego, CA.

Published by Reflections Publishing LLC
© 2023, 2024 Reflections Publishing LLC. All rights reserved.

No part of this book may be used or reproduced in any manner whatsoever without the prior written permission of the publisher, except for brief quotations embodied in critical articles and reviews.

Disclaimer of Warranties/Limitation of Liability: The publisher and the author make no representations or warranties, express or implied, with respect to this book, including without limitation the accuracy or completeness of the content thereof, and the publisher and the author each specifically disclaim any and all such representations or warranties, including without limitation any warranty of title, merchantability, non-infringement, and/or fitness for a particular purpose. No warranty may be created or extended by any sales or promotional materials. The advice and strategies contained in this book may not be suitable for every person and/or every situation. This book is sold with the understanding that the publisher and the author are not engaged in rendering medical, legal, or other professional advice or services. If professional assistance is required, the services of a competent professional should be sought. Neither the publisher nor the author shall be liable for any damages or losses arising in any way from this book and/or the content thereof. The fact that an individual, organization, or website is referred to in this book as a citation and/or potential source of further information does not mean that the publisher or the author endorses any information or recommendation that the individual, organization, or the website may provide. In addition, readers should be aware that any website listed in this book may have changed or disappeared between when this work was written/published and when it is read. While the author has made every effort to provide accurate telephone numbers and/or internet addresses at the time of publication, neither the publisher nor the author assume any responsibility for errors or for changes that occur after publication. The publisher and the author do not have any control over and do not assume any responsibility for third-party websites or their content.

Neither the publisher nor the author is engaged in rendering professional medical advice or services, including without limitation to any individual reader. The ideas, information, and/or suggestions contained in this book are not intended as a substitute for consulting with your physician and/or other professional service provider. All matters regarding your health require medical supervision. Neither the author nor the publisher shall be liable or responsible for any damages or losses allegedly arising from any ideas, information, suggestions, and/or other content in this book.

Names, characters, businesses, organizations, places, events, and incidents included in this book either are the product of the author's imagination or are used fictitiously. Any resemblance to actual persons, living or dead, events, or locales is entirely coincidental.

First Edition. Published in the United States of America.

Paperback ISBN: 978-1-61660-018-1

Visit our website at www.reflectionspublishing.com for more information or inquiries

* * *

The photograph on the cover was taken at Torrey Pines State Park in San Diego, California.

APA Formatting and Style Guide (7th Edition) was utilized for citations.

The fonts used in this playbook are **Ad Lib** (section headers and page headers), Times New Roman (body copy), and Futura Condensed (Appendix body copy).

Table of Contents

Introduction **1, 3**
Preface i: *The Resilience Game Plan* **School-based Intervention Program** **3**
    • Schools Are the Key 4
Preface ii: *The Resilience Game Plan* **Facilitator's Readiness Tool Kit** **7**
    • Initiatives for Cultivating Overall Student Success 8
    • Student Understanding Goals (UG) and Performance Goals (PG) 9
    • *The Resilience Game Plan* Facilitator's Readiness Tool Kit 12
    • *The Resilience Game Plan* Facilitator's Readiness Tool Kit Worksheet 16
Section One: *The Resilience Game Plan* **Pre-Assessment** **19, 5**
    • How to Analyze *The Resilience Game Plan* Pre- and Post-Assessments 20-23, 6-7
Section Two: Reflections Publishing Communication Assessment **25, 9**
Section Three: How *The Resilience Game Plan* **Will Benefit You** **27, 11**
Section Four: How to Become a Resilent Global Changemaker **31, 15**
Section Five: How to Use *The Resilience Game Plan* **33, 17**
    • Six Strategies for Success 34, 18
    • Creating Your "Personalized Game Plan" 34-35, 18-19
    • How to Use *The Resilience Game Plan* 36-56, 20-42

   4114U Life Topic Pages **36, 20**
   Playbook Strategy #1: Understanding Brain Power **36, 20**
   Playbook Strategy #2: Learning Cognitive Skills **38, 22**
       • Step One: Expressive Writing 38-40, 22-24
       • Step Two: Gauging Your Emotions - Subjective Units of Distress Scale 41, 25
       • Step Three: Overcoming Obstacles - Fear and Avoidance Hierarchy Ladder ... 42, 26
   Playbook Strategy #3: Learning Communication Skills **43, 27**
       - Compliments and Praise 43, 27
       - Feeling Respected 43, 27
       - Friendliness and Caring 43, 28
       - Helping Hand 44, 28
       - Hugs 44, 28
       - Spending Time Together 44, 28
       - Token of Friendship/Gift-Giving 44, 28
       - Unconditional Love 44, 29
   Playbook Strategy #4: Learning Mindfulness Skills **45, 30**
   Playbook Strategy #5: Developing New Habits **46, 31**
       • Well-Being Game Plan • Well-Being Habit Tracker: **47, 33**
          - Sleep 48, 34
          - Exercise 49, 35
          - Mindfulness 50, 36
          - Nature 51, 37
          - Hydration 52, 38
          - Nutrition .... 53, 38 MS/39 HS
          - Social Fitness 53, 39
          - Caring 54, 40

* **Facilitator's Guide Pages**   **Student Edition Pages**

- Gratitude	54, 40
- Happiness	54, 40
- Laugh	55, 41
- Smile	55, 41
- Music	55, 41
Playbook Strategy #6: Setting Goals and Reducing Anxiety	**56, 42**
Section Six: What's Your Game Plan? • Warm-up	**57, 43**
- Academic Pressures	58, 44
- Habit Formation: Forming New Habits and Breaking Old Habits	60, 50
- What is Your Legacy? - Core Values	62, 56
- Who Are Your Mentors/Coaches?	64, 62
Section Seven: What's Your Game Plan? • Life Choices	**67, 69**
- Self and Identity	68, 70
- Social Media - Setting Boundaries	70, 76
- Time Management - Life Balance	72, 82
Section Eight: What's Your Game Plan? • Life Crises	**75, 89**
- Abuse - Domestic, Physical, and Verbal	76, 90
- Anxiety	78, 96
- Depression	80, 102
- Self-Harm	82, 108
- Substance Abuse - Alcohol and Drugs	84, 114
Section Nine: What's Your Game Plan? • Relationships	**87, 121**
- Bullying/Cyberbullying	88, 122
- Caregiver (Parent or Guardian)	90, 128
- Friendship	92, 134
- Peer Pressure	94, 140
Section Ten: *The Resilience Game Plan* Post-Assessment	**97, 147**
- Post-Assessment	98-99, 148-149
Section Eleven: 4114U - Appendix	**101, 151**
• Depression Game Plan	102, 152
• Nutrition Game Plan	103, 153
• Sample Competency-Based Grading Operating Procedures	104-105
• Brain Power Color Chart	106, 154
• *The Resilience Game Plan* Evidence-Based Intervention Program	107
Section Twelve: 4114U - Notes	**155**
Section Thirteen: 4114U - Glossary of Terms	**169**
Section Fourteen: 4114U - Resources	**171**
Section Fifteen: 4114U - Supplemental References, References	**109, 175**
Create-Your-Own Life Topic	**188-193**
Space to Download and Process Your Thoughts	**194**
***The Resilience Game Plan* Certificate of Completion**	**195**

* **Facilitator's Guide Pages**   **Student Edition Pages**

• Introduction •

Dear Reader,

Until a few years ago, admitting students had mental health challenges such as depression, suicidal ideation, anxiety, or eating disorders was seen as taboo. The challenges and others related to students' social and emotional wellness were only to be discussed with pediatricians, therapists, and maybe school counselors. Students lucky enough to have the family resources or districts with dedicated therapists, like Licensed Marriage and Family Therapists (LMFTs), were generally provided the invaluable care that may have saved their lives and/or provided them with the skills to be successful students.

The U.S. Surgeon General, Dr. Vivek Murthy shared that teen mental health has reached crisis and endemic levels (US Surgeon General Advisory Report, 2021). He said that mental health challenges are the leading cause of disability and poor life outcomes in young people. He further reported that in recent years, we have seen a significant increase in certain mental health disorders in youth—noting the aforementioned: depression, anxiety, and suicidal ideation.

In a partnership with Challenge Success, Donahue (2021) with NBC News reported on their research study highlighting three key findings:

- Students, especially females and students of color, continue to experience high levels of stress and pressure.
- Student engagement with learning, which is always a challenge, is especially low.
- Students' relationships with adults and peers are strong, yet appear strained at times.

This means that many students are struggling to maintain healthy relationships with peers and adults, to perform well in school, and to experience happiness and joy. Strong social and emotional skills are necessary not only to ensure students do well in school, have self efficacy, but are also needed to grow into productive adults. Ensuring that students have resiliency skills, specifically cognitive, communication, and mindfulness skills to develop strong mental, social and emotional wellness, is critical to their overall and future success.

The OECD 2030 Life Skills Study found the following:

Achievement at school depends on a number of social and emotional skills, such as perseverance, self-control, responsibility, curiosity, and emotional stability. Some social and emotional skills are a prerequisite for successful participation and performance in academic settings. Moreover, while cognitive skills have long been considered the most important determinants of success in employment, recent studies show that social and emotional skills also directly affect occupational status and income. In fact, in some cases, social and emotional skills are equally, if not more so, as important as cognitive skills in determining future employment.

Responses to these findings require an "All in Village" effort; hence, ensuring the mental health of our adolescents requires collaboration—schools, policymakers, families, institutions, and individuals—and a commitment to how we view, prioritize, and address mental health.

As a high school principal of mostly first-generation college-bound students with numerous challenges stemming primarily from poverty and the pandemic, I had young folks who could barely find their way to the schoolhouse gates—due to the trauma they had experienced in one form or another. We were lucky at my school though because we had one of the best LMFTs and generally two LMFT interns on staff. Because we were a small school with two entrances, we could look every student in the eye each morning to check their readiness to learn (mental state) and provide real-time support. We were fortunate enough to provide support to not only individual students, but also to their families and our teaching staff.

Being superintendent of an affluent secondary school district gave me a window into the challenges of students who are constantly under pressure to perform and, in some cases, by any means necessary. Sometimes this led to students' self-harm, attempting to take their lives and, unfortunately, in a few cases succeeding. What struck me was that the number one and two districts in the state at the time both had some of the highest suicide rates in the state. The Psychiatric Emergency Response Team (PERT) was called to our high-performing high schools several times a month. Although we cannot pinpoint the exact numbers, we also had a group of students who regularly engaged in self-harm with cutting.

One analysis of self-injury across more than 40 countries discovered (Recovery Village, 2023):

- About 17% of all people will self-harm during their lifetime.
- The average age of the first incident of self-harm is 13.
- 45% of people use cutting as their method of self-injury.
- About 50% of people seek help for their self-harm, but only from friends instead of professionals.

Having LMFTs at every school and/or parents who can afford services for their children is ideal, but unrealistic. Therefore, we need a way to get ahead of the crises by providing students with a systematic means to manage their mental, social and emotional wellness and prevent crises. An effective structured plan promoting self-efficacy and productive ways to address possible mental health crises is needed—before they become a crisis.

The author of *The Resilience Game Plan*, Colleen Ster, understands the challenges facing students and is determined to find a way to address them. *The Resilience Game Plan* is a way to do just that. In fact, adults who reviewed *The Resilience Game Plan* have reported how reading the book was helpful to them and other adults as well, not just students.

Everyone needs a game plan for dealing with life's difficulties, especially adolescents regarding ways to address social, emotional, and even physical challenges in a healthy manner and before reaching crisis levels. Using *The Resilience Game Plan* is a viable solution to building our students' repertoire of such tools.

Wishing you all the best,

Cheryl James-Ward, Ed.D.

Cheryl James-Ward has been a Superintendent of Schools, Schools CEO, Director of Academics and Innovation, elementary school principal, vice principal, math teacher and NASA software engineer.

Preface
i

The Resilience Game Plan: School-based Intervention Program

• Schools Are the Key •

Even before the pandemic, adolescent mental health disorders were a global public health crisis (Patel et al., 2007). Additionally, **mental health disorders** (i.e., diagnosed psychiatric conditions, as well as subclinical behavioral symptoms, socioemotional afflictions, and suicidal risk) **are linked to numerous adverse short- and long-term academic, economic, physical health, and social ramifications** (Jokela et al., 2009; Greenberg et al., 2015; Soneson et al., 2020; Vigo, Thornicroft & Atun, 2016). Furthermore, early intervention methods have proven significant results in decreasing psychological disorders (Children and Young People's Mental Health and Wellbeing Taskforce, 2015; Fazel et al., 2014; National Health Service England, 2016); however, less than 30% of adolescents receive mental health treatment (Eklund & Dowdy, 2014). Many students, even if they want to receive treatment for their mental health, experience numerous barriers (i.e., insurance woes, travel hindrances, cost obstacles, and a wait-list for first-time patients) in receiving evidence-based psychological treatments (Gratzer & Khalid-Khan, 2016; Nordh et al., 2021).

Research supports the implementation of intervention methods (i.e., teaching mental and emotional regulation skills), as these techniques will assist adolescents to excel in their academic performance and develop prosocial behavior (Urry et al., 2006). As you will find in *The Resilience Game Plan: The Playbook for Developing Cognitive, Communication, and Mindfulness Life Skills* (*The RGP*), when these techniques are taught with repetitive practice, these skills likely become automatic habits (Fischer & Bidell, 1998). This *RGP Facilitator's Guide* can be utilized by a parent/guardian or in a psychologist or counselor's office. However, due to the amount of time students spend at school, we cannot ignore the fact that schools play a significant role in cultivating the necessary cognitive and socioemotional skills that adolescents need to lead productive and content lives (Heckman, 2007).

School-based programs continue to be the channel showing the most promise and significant results in reaching the majority of adolescents while also identifying mental health disorders. Schools have the ability to focus on identifying at-risk youth while also adding social validity (Green et al., 2022). Social validity is deemed a crucial key to the puzzle because for a school-based program to succeed, the surrounding community needs to place a value on the program's recommended goals, methods, and outcomes. By supporting the feasibility, acceptability, and implementation of the program, it has long-term sustainability (Humphrey & Wigelsworth, 2016). **Since educators spend numerous hours with their students and most mental health disorders are often triggered during the puberty years, schools are in the best position to help identify at-risk youth and implement prevention and intervention techniques for early detection** (Department of Health and Department for Education, 2017)—potentially reversing any psychiatric symptoms (Cole et al., 2011; Nouretdinov et al., 2011; Rao & Chen, 2009; Scher et al., 2004; Teicher & Samson, 2016; Tymofiyeva et al., 2020).

Adolescents worldwide are looking for ways to cope and maneuver in this pandemic-changed world; thus, students and families are more receptive to treatment options and intervention strategies to help them deal with their anxiety, depression, social isolation, loneliness, and fear of ongoing disease risk and future exposure (Behan, 2020; Gordon et al., 2021). Moreover, **the United States Preventative Services Task Force (USPSTF) stated that screening for depression and suicide risk is essential for the 12- to 18-years-old age group** (Bitsko et al., 2022; USPSTF, October 22, 2022), as adolescence is a known time for the onset of psychiatric disorders and a crucial period to implement intervention strategies (Selemon & Zecevic,

2015). Due to this pressing need and newfound adolescent receptivity to mental health interventions, *The RGP* is created explicitly for this age group—making *The RGP* a good investment for students' short- and long-term mental and physical health outcomes.

Since early adolescence is identified as a time when teenagers display a gender disparity regarding negative opinions on mental health struggles and receptiveness to receiving treatment, research indicates that beginning education on mental health issues in middle school is the opportune time (Chandra & Minkovitz, 2006); however, if your middle school did not start a mental health intervention initiative, then we recommend you get started right away.

• Community Involvement

With all populations affected by the pandemic, the goal is to involve parents and the community to help the student learner address any stigma attached to mental health issues and overcome possible learning challenges of students' receptiveness to receiving treatment (Bueno-Notivol et al., 2021; Chandra & Minkovitz, 2006).

• Equipping You With the Tools You Need

Our goal with *The RGP Facilitator's Guide* is to provide opportunities for schools/districts to develop common language and standard operating procedures so that educators feel adequately equipped to step into this space. After reading through *The RGP*, educators should feel confident to assess and identify students struggling with mental health disorders (Day et al., 2017; Evans et al., 2017; Evans & Hurrell, 2016). *The RGP* is an effective advisory or homeroom curriculum tool which provides school faculty and students a "How to Use *The RGP*" training section. The intervention tips and tools (i.e., cognitive behavior therapy techniques, communication activities, mindfulness meditation methods, self-reflection exercises, role-playing scripts, and journaling pages) create a supportive learning space for students to process their anxiety, emotions, and stress. While students may have some knowledge of the strategies in *The RGP*, teens will benefit from the coaching methods of repeatedly practicing and addressing any knowledge gaps, gaining confidence and motivation in learning and applying new skills in a safe environment; additionally, students will be learning some new habits and unlearning some bad habits along the way (Dirksen, 2016).

• The Bottom Line

Research has shown that if mental health issues are not resolved and left untreated in adolescents, then the trajectory of a child's brain development is altered; hence, this is a crucial time to identify at-risk youth and **implement intervention strategies and hope for reversal of psychiatric symptoms** (Cole et al., 2011; Nouretdinov et al., 2011; Scher et al., 2004; Teicher & Samson, 2016; Tymofiyeva et al., 2020). As students complete *The RGP* playbook—learning new skills along the way (i.e., cognitive, communication, and mindfulness techniques), the assessments in *The RGP* can potentially assist clinicians in developing effective treatment plans to achieve the most robust clinical outcome (Cole et al., 2011).

• Confidentiality and Family Educational Rights and Privacy Act (FERPA)

Please note that the information your students present in *The RGP* is confidential. Only when students present a threat to themselves or others should this information be shared with anyone. Otherwise, students' privacy is to be respected under the federal FERPA.

Preface
ii

The Resilience Game Plan: Facilitator's Readiness Tool Kit

• Initiatives for Cultivating Overall Student Success •

Easy as 1-2-3:

1. Prior to implementing *The Resilience Game Plan: The Playbook for Developing Cognitive, Communication, and Mindfulness Life Skills (The RGP)* with adolescents, we encourage you to utilize *The RGP* Facilitator's Readiness Tool Kit provided in this *Facilitator's Guide*. This document provides step-by-step instructions to ensure your school has a plan in place to help identify and support at-risk students.

2. Before your students start the playbook, have them take *The RGP* Pre-Assessment. This gives you a baseline and helps to potentially identify any at-risk students. Next, utilizing your personal copy of *The RGP: Student Edition,* have your students take the Reflections Publishing Communication Assessment and walk them through the "How to Use *The RGP*" section. As your learners create new habits from *The RGP*, you can begin by teaching them how to have a growth mindset in the "How *The RGP* Will Benefit You" section. Lastly, students are told throughout the playbook that if they find any information listed in this workbook upsetting, they should talk to a parent/guardian/care giver, trusted adult, school counselor, teacher, or medical professional.

3. Now, create a public relations campaign to set the tone for your school's stance on mental health:
   - Send a press release to school and area newspapers.
   - Email parent(s)/guardian(s)/caregiver(s) an update on implementing *The RGP*, along with talking points of [Topics] learned at school so they can discuss at home. (Parent/Guardian/Caregiver resources are available on the ReflectionsPublishing.com website.) Have them take the Reflections Publishing Communication Assessment so they can share their "Preferred Method of Communication" with their child.
   - Notify local businesses on how you are implementing *The RGP* to improve your students' mental and physical health. Businesses may provide resources to motivate and help celebrate the completion of *The RGP* playbook.
   - No reason to reinvent the wheel. Send in ways to encourage and share your school's success stories using *The RGP* with your students to cster@reflectionspublishing.com.

Ensure Your School's Success

At schools where Dr. Ward has been principal, it has always been helpful to start with common language and practices to support students who show signs of anxiety, depression, and/or self-harm. This means bringing the entire school staff together (e.g., educators and support staff) to create or update *The RGP* Facilitator's Readiness Tool Kit and the necessary steps to take when confronted with at-risk students. Schools can create teams to collaborate around the plan, but ultimately, the entire staff must come together to understand, commit, and support students with the specific language and practices. As new personnel are onboarded, it is important to provide them with the necessary training for continuity.

Once common language and practices have been determined, you are ready to start using *The RGP*. The goal is for all students and staff to use the same terminology and have the same next steps to assist students who are in distress. As students move throughout their day, they should be able to expect the same responses and support from all staff. It should not be left to chance to receive the appropriate care. We encourage you to revisit your *The RGP* Facilitator's Readiness Tool Kit annually with staff to ensure you are always on the same page.

• Student Understanding Goals and Performance Goals •

Core principles from the growth mindset theory, self-regulation theory, learning theory, experiential learning theory, and sociocultural learning theory are utilized in *The RGP*. These theories contain skills and a framework of knowledge with the benefit of long-term, brain-based retention and retrieval of newly-stored information (Schmidt & Bjork, 2017). *The RGP* is written with a motivational voice of a life coach and upon completion of *The RGP*, learners should have mastered the following skill sets.

The following concepts are found in *The RGP Evidence-Based Intervention Program* in the Appendix on page 107 and are beneficial to all *RGP* Facilitators (educators, counselors, parents, psychologists, etc.) who are passionate to work with tweens, teens, and emerging young adults.

Learning Theory Pedagogical Strategies	Understanding Goals (UG)	Performance Goals (PG)
Retrieval Practice/Examination: A formal assessment of knowledge (Rosenberg et al., 2022)	Students will understand they will take *The RGP* Pre-Assessment before starting the playbook on week 1, and *The RGP* Post-Assessment at the end of the semester (week 15). This provides the facilitator a baseline on week 1 to assess the cognitive, communication, and mindfulness skills learned by the end of the semester.	Students will examine their results from their *Resilience Game Plan* Pre- and Post-Assessments with their facilitator and devise a game plan where the student is an active participant in creating their strategy (Dirksen, 2016).
Learning Theory	**Understanding Goals (UG)**	**Performance Goals (PG)**
Growth Mindset Theory	Learners will discover that by developing a growth mindset they set themselves onto a positive trajectory for both learning and motivation in difficult life scenarios (Yeager & Dweck, 2012).	1. Students with a growth mindset are potentially more equipped to overcome challenges in their personal life, as well as maintain a strong academic performance. (Butterfield, Lamb, Good, & Dweck, 2006). 2. Learners will commit to their educational growth and remain eager to learn for the love of learning (Claro et al., 2016; Haimovitz & Dweck, 2017).
Learning Theory	**Understanding Goals (UG)**	**Performance Goals (PG)**
Social Cognitive Theory (Bandura, 2004)	Learners will understand and exhibit prosocial behaviors and moral development as they grow. These improvements will positively affect them cognitively on an individual, environmental, and societal level. (Li et al., 2022).	1. Learners will work on themselves to add social value (İrengün, O., & Arıkboğa, 2015). 2. Adolescents will thrive due to their connectedness, good health, resilience, academic skills, and supportive environment to reach their full potential (Guthold et al., 2023).

Experiential Learning Theory	Understanding Goals (UG)	Performance Goals (PG)
Learning Through Experience: When knowledge transforms a person via the transformation of experience (Kolb, 1984)	Learners will understand that knowledge is a result of the combination of grasping and transforming experience (Kolb, 1984).	Students will learn tips and tools through collaborative learning. Learners will conduct face-to-face interviews and activities with their advisory or homeroom teacher to discuss skills learned in *The Resilience Game Plan*. When students are trained with Experiential Learning methods, it increases motivation and engagement (Mater, Daher, & Mahamid, 2023).
Learning Theory Pedagogical Strategies	Understanding Goals (UG)	Performance Goals (PG)
Interleave Instruction: A learning strategy that mixes several concepts during one learning session (Rosenberg et al., 2022)	Learners will understand how to "connect the dots" and learn instrinsic content with a bit of friction which will help them to remember their new skills (Sweller, 1988).	1. The learner will reach their goals interweaving multiple intervention methods (i.e., CBT, mindfulness, and mediation activities); and 2. The student will learn various strategies in multiple ways to alleviate their anxiety and stress (Rohrer, Dedrick, & Burgess, 2014). 3. Student will increase their performance and ability to assimilate new material using color-coding methods (e.g., *The RGP* Brain Power Color Chart) as they learn the areas of the brain affected by each life topic (Zavaruieva, Bondarenko, & Kedko, 2022).
Self-Affirmation (Cascio et al., 2016)	The learner is motivated to have a positive self-view and increase well-being	The learner will work on reflecting on their core values and practicing positive "I am statements" to promote their self-worth.
Spaced Instruction: Obtain a specific skill or set of skills over a period of time (Rosenberg et al., 2022)	The learner understands the research that spaced learning supports a better long-term retention of the material (Bjork & Bjork, 2011; Schmidt & Bjork, 2017).	1. Adolescents will learn CBT skills and be introduced to interpersonal processing techniques that are reexamined and practiced numerous times during the training process. 2. Students will utilize journaling pages as an expressive journal-writing section to download and process their anxiety, emotions, and stressful thoughts (McAdams, 2018; Pennebaker, 2018).
Variability of Learning Contexts: Consolidating contextual variability avenues (i.e., physical settings and teaching methods) (Rosenberg et al., 2022)	1. Learners will understand that when they master new knowledge in various physical environments they are able to retrieve and utilize these new skills more effectively (Smith, 1984). 2. Students will understand that learning Cognitive Behavior Therapy (CBT) skills can help them achieve their goals.	1. Learners will study their new CBT skills in different environments to help them retain this new knowledge. 2. Through didactic, structured coaching, the student learns the teaching method that will help them achieve their goals. 3. Role-playing exercises in small groups will engrain in the learner new material through movement and verbal interactions. 4. The learner exercises their newfound CBT knowledge in a mock session that is overseen by the group participants (Rosenberg et al., 2022).

Self-Regulation Theory	Understanding Goals (UG)	Performance Goals (PG)
Strength Model of Self-Regulation	Learners will understand that self-regulation includes starting and maintaining behavioral change, suppressing unwanted behaviors, and not acknowledging negative demands (Heatherton, 2010).	1. Learners will work towards becoming good group members where they may alter their behaviors, thoughts, feelings, or actions to meet their personal goals and maintain societal standards (Heatherton, 2010; Baumeister & Heatherton, 1996). 2. By initiating self-regulatory efforts, these positive changes will help learners reach their goals (Heatherton, 2010). 3. Students will achieve their goals by learning to manage their "personal gas tanks."
Socio-Cultural Learning Theory	**Understanding Goals (UG)**	**Performance Goals (PG)**
Internalization of Verbal Guidance: Method for a child to gain new knowledge in collaboration and through guided practice from a more knowledgeable individual (Vygotsky, 1978)	Learners will understand they are active participants in learning their culture and they must educate themselves with the necessary tools (Miller, 2016).	Learners are encouraged to find five coaches and/or mentors in their life that they respect, are eager to learn from, and more knowledgeable than themselves; this private, inner speech is part of the developmental process that differentiates one's ability to self-regulate versus being regulated by others to help reach their goals (Miller, 2016; Winsler, Fernyhough, & Montero, 2009).
Zone of Proximal Development (ZPD): Method created so a child can gain new knowledge in collaboration and through guided practice from a more knowledgeable and competent individual (Vygotsky, 1978)	Learners will incorporate the method of scaffolding where new information and skills are stored in memory, so learner can access this knowledge in a future setting (Churcher, Downs, & Tewksbury, 2014).	1. Learners will have this framework of CBT, meditation, and mindfulness skills to access when needed (i.e., dealing with a stressful situation) (Shvarts & Bakker, 2019). 2. Learners will utilize scaffolding to build temporary frameworks when learning new skills (Churcher, Downs, & Tewksbury, 2014). 3. The goal is for the learner to collaborate with their mentor while structuring the social interaction, so they are active learners (Miller, 2016). 4. The skilled adult is continually assessing the child learner and making adjustments based on the child's prior and newly-gained knowledge (Miller, 2016).
Guided Use of Object Substitutions: (Vygotsky, 1978)	Learners will understand how mental functions (i.e., analytical reasoning, attention, creative imagination, emotions, memory, moral reasoning, and will) use consciously-directed moral reasoning in the construction/reconstruction of self-identity in their lifetime (Smolucha & Smolucha, 2020).	Learners will gain skills to implement these theories to provide a framework to address how they can best learn and retain skills in a collaborative social environment interpsychologically (i.e., with others) and also intrapsychologically (i.e., internal mechanism within the adolescent)—with the ultimate goal of helping them succeed (Churcher, Downs, & Tewksbury, 2014; Cole, 1986, John-Steiner & Mahn, 1996).

• *The Resilience Game Plan* Facilitator's Readiness Tool Kit •

Below you will find some of the areas that we addressed or would encourage you to consider when working on your Game Plan Safety Strategies for Student Wellness.

• Ways to Reduce Academic Pressures:

Reducing Academic Pressures	School Calendars: • Moving Up School Start Dates • Study Free Vacations • Finals Before Winter Break	In the district where I was superintendent, the first day of school was moved to earlier in the summer so that students would finish semester one finals before the winter holidays. This allowed students real vacations, those in which they weren't stressed over completing reports or studying for upcoming exams.
	Bell Schedules	In 2022, after longstanding research showed the negative impact of early start times on teens, the California State Board of Education mandated a later start time for high schools and middle schools—with high school starting no earlier than 8:30 and middle schools no earlier than 8:00 AM. Bell schedules across the state were then adjusted to meet the mandates.
	School Sports	As a result of the later start time, athletic practices and games were also revised to later in the day. At the onset, districts with widespread bussing were in a panic and athletic directors across the state balked because this meant later evenings for games and practices. San Diego Unified, a large district with bussing, pivoted well and is a good example of success.
Culture and Climate	Sense of Belonging	The culture and climate of the school sits at its core. How are students welcomed onto the campus each day? Do they have a sense of belonging? If yes, what specifically can this be attributed to? If not, what needs to be done to ensure that all kids feel welcomed. Where Dr. Ward was charter school CEO, teachers, called learning facilitators, met students at the door each period. School personnel met students as they entered campus every morning with a warm welcome and a check for readiness to learn. They spent the first two weeks of the school year reviewing The e3 Way, including school-wide and classroom community, before school, lunch, passing period, and after school etiquette. Students learned how to leave a positive footprint in the digital world and how to work together using the motto, "Take care of you, Take care of each other, Take care of e3. Once monthly an e3 Way assembly was held focusing on: mental and social wellness, celebrations, financial wellness and campus updates. Affinity clubs and/or the student council ran all major student functions.

Master Schedules	Course Offerings	At e3, the master schedule was based on student interests (in addition to the required state courses per grade level). When singletons requested courses that were not on the schedule, online offerings through UC Scouts and/or Engenuity were utilized. With the influx of online curricula, meeting individual student needs has been made easy. At e3, every student was given access to every course and supported as necessary. In addition to the required courses, students were provided with community college dual and concurrent enrollment opportunities and AP offerings. (It is important to note that the more AP courses your school offers, the more students will need to take to compete with schoolmates in the college process.)
Grading Policies	No Grade Less than 50%	At one of our schools, the grading policy was revised in line with a 1-5 Rubric and no score less than a 50% (aligned with the decimal scale for grades A-D).
	Next-Steps Grading Guide	A student grading guide with suggestions for next steps given a grade of: A, B, C, or IP.
	Competency-Based Grading	Grades based on reaching a certain competency rather than time bound. Additional opportunities for students to learn and retake exams to demonstrate competency (i.e., like when you take a driving test, you get to retake it until you reach competency). (See Appendix *The RGP* Competency-based Grading)
Assessments	Multiple Opportunities to Demonstrate Competency	Using competency based grading students are given many opportunities to pass exams with interventions and data analysis in between exams.
	Individualized Student Data	Provide students with real-time electronic data so they know their scores/grades in any course or intervention in near real-time. Today, with artificial intelligence and real-time smart assessments, it is easier for districts to provide students with a myriad of data points to manage their progress. This requires a robust data system and training for students, teachers, and parents regarding how to use the information.
Design Thinking/ Project Based Learning	Processes for Solving Real World Problems	At one of our high schools, all students utilized Design Thinking, a five-step process requiring creativity and critical thinking to solve real problems. Student groups were annually recognized or awarded prizes from the national organization, Project Invent, or MIT for outstanding design thinking projects.

Academics	Revised Homework Policies	Because our charter organization transitioned to competency-based grading; homework took a back seat being only worth 10% of the total course grade and students recognizing the purpose of homework was to improve and expand one's learning/knowledge. Completing homework became important to learning and mastery, rather than a chore.
	Voice and Choice	At one of our high schools, we worked with a team to create a new way of teaching and learning called Voice and Choice which allowed students to have self-efficacy in their own education. After lunch, students would be the architects of their learning by designing how to use their afternoon time. This included opportunities for community college dual enrollment, internships, study time, tutoring, design thinking projects, e-sports, wealth-building sessions, and more. Students had the opportunity to redesign their afternoon learning weekly.
	Faculty Development and Sustainability	At the charter organization, we utilized student-assessment data of all types (e.g., attendance, discipline; out of class, classroom assessments, benchmark, intervention assessments, NWEA and MAP) as well as data from our collaborative classroom observations to determine professional development.
	Parent Education	To support students, grade-level parent meetings with information regarding ways to support their students were held. Saturday Parent Collaboratives were opportunities to learn more about how teenagers work and support teens. University led parent nights were another layer of supporting teens, understanding the teen brain, ways to help teens enjoy high school, and preparing for college.

- **Game Plan to Address:**
  - **Abuse (Domestic, Physical, and Verbal)**
  - **Anxiety**
  - **Bullying and Cyberbullying**
  - **Depression**
  - **Substance Abuse (Alcohol and Drugs)**
  - **Self-Harm**

Even though a school's primary purpose is academics, the reality is that school faculty also assists in students' personal, social, and mental health. According to Weston, Morris, and Williams (2018) in an article written in the American School Counselor Assocciation called Nonsuicidal Self-Injury in the Schools: A Tiered Prevention Approach for Reducing Social Contagion, they suggest the following intervention strategies:

1. Clearly communicate to students who and where they should go to at school to seek help.

2. Introduce school staff members to students so they are more familiar with the person they are going to talk to as they address their health and safety concerns (i.e., bullying, cutting, self-harm, and suicide).

3. Ask school staff if they still need more support and resources to address self-harm cases among students.

4. Conduct staff training in how to:
   - Define and explain Suicidal Self-Harm (SSH) and Nonsuicidal Self-Injury (NSSI);
   - Identify warning signs of SSH and NSSI;
   - Respond to students if Self-Harm or NSSI is suspected and/or evidence is seen;
   - Provide students with coping tips and tools—specific to their situation; and
   - Create a follow-up plan to fully support the student.

If students find any information listed in the playbook triggering or upsetting, they are encouraged to talk to a trusted adult, school counselor, teacher, parent, or medical professional. Therefore, when filling out *The Resilience Game Plan* Facilitor's Readiness Tool Kit Worksheet, make sure your school has procedures in place to address all of these scenarios (i.e., assisting a student with anxiety, depression, or self-harm ideation).

• *The Resilience Game Plan*
Facilitator's Readiness Tool Kit Worksheet •

Ways to Reduce Academic Pressures:

1. _____
2. _____
3. _____
4. _____
5. _____
6. _____
7. _____
8. _____
9. _____
10. _____
11. _____
12. _____
13. _____
14. _____
15. _____
16. _____
17. _____
18. _____
19. _____
20. _____
21. _____
22. _____
23. _____
24. _____
25. _____

How to Combat Extensive Social Media Use:

1. _____
2. _____
3. _____
4. _____
5. _____

Steps to Take When Abuse is Suspected (i.e., Domestic, Physical, and Verbal):

1. _____
2. _____
3. _____
4. _____
5. _____

How to Combat Anxious Students:

1. _____
2. _____
3. _____
4. _____
5. _____

Steps to Take When a Student is Identified as Suffering from Depression:

1. _____
2. _____
3. _____
4. _____
5. _____

Steps to Take When Substance Abuse is Suspected (i.e., Alcohol and Drug):

1. _____
2. _____
3. _____
4. _____
5. _____

Steps to Take When Self-Harm is Suspected - Cutting:

1. _____
2. _____
3. _____
4. _____
5. _____

Steps to Take When Self-Harm is Suspected - Suicide:

1. _____
2. _____
3. _____
4. _____
5. _____

Create School-wide Statement on Stance Against Bullying/Cyberbullying/Peer Pressure:

1. _____
2. _____
3. _____
4. _____
5. _____

Steps to Take Regarding Family and/or Guardian Issues:

1. _____
2. _____
3. _____
4. _____
5. _____

Additional Notes:

Section One

The Resilience Game Plan Pre-Assessment

(Page 5 in *The RGP: Student Edition*)

FOR LESSON PLANNING PURPOSES - AMOUNT OF TIME TO ALLOCATE TO TAKE PRE-ASSESSMENT: 5 minutes

*Student Edition Pages

• How to Analyze *The Resilience Game Plan* Pre- and Post-Assessments •

Before jumping into the *The Resilience Game Plan: The Playbook for Developing Cognitive, Communication, and Mindfulness Life Skills (The RGP)* curriculum, have your students take the following Pre-Asssessment (i.e., week one). This ensures you will have a baseline for your students in regards to each topic included in the playbook. If you want to do a "Mid-semester Assessment," (i.e., week seven). then you can go to the www.reflectionspublishing.com website and download a blank version of *The RGP* Self-Assessment. Otherwise, at the end of the semester, have your students go to **Section Ten - page 147** in their playbook and take an end-of-the semester *RGP* Post-Assessment (i.e., week 15).

• Universal Screening

This assessment will utilize Universal Screening components as students are assessed via self-reported measures to help identify students needing mental health support (Harrell-Williams et al., 2015; Kamphaus & Reynolds, 2007).

• The Purpose

One purpose of the student self-assessment is to help you to identify any potential at-risk students. As mentioned earlier, the Department of Health and Department for Education (2017) encourage you to immediately provide any necessary support to offset potential mental health disorders. The second purpose for the student self-assessment is to provide a baseline for students as they begin to build their game plan.

• Design Strategy

Student information is collected in the same categories that student learners are familiar with in *The RGP*. Instead of giving students twenty or more different screening tests, *The RGP* Assessment incorporates many constructs, components, and variables in tests such as the Adverse Childhood Experiences (ACES) assessment (Benedetti et al., 2014; Burke Harris, 2018) and the Beck Depression Inventory (BDI) tests (Beck, Steer, & Garbin 1988). With students taking just one short assessment, you should be able to gather the crucial data needed to help start identifying possible at-risk students in your classroom.

• What to Watch For

While questions regarding the student's engagement in school and their peer group also provide essential data, the area to closely analyze in The RGP Pre- and Post-Assessments is the "What's Your Game Plan? • Life Crises" section. This section is highlighted in yellow and provides crucial data because if the student indicates "Yes" for any of these questions, these situations can cause negative alterations in their brain. The "Social Media" and "Bullying/Cyberbullying areas are also highlighted in a lighter yellow because these two categories can also identify at-risk students who might potentially inflict self-harm on themselves. Questions regarding the "Students' Subjective Well-Being" are also highlighted as it could possibly be another indicator that a student is struggling. **The goal is for you to identify a potentially at-risk student, and then your intervention will hopefully offset future health issues, such as depression** (Tymofiyeva et al., 2020).

- **Why the Urgency?**

Research has shown the connection between an adolescent's long-term psychological prognosis and the benefit of interventions; therefore, getting a game plan like *The RGP* into the hands of adolescents is key. Furthermore, with the prevalence of depression and mental health challenges emerging post the COVID-19 outbreak, an equal playing field has now surfaced—validating the need for evidence-based interventions for all individuals (Gordon et al., 2021). With the channel of school-based programs showing significant results in identifying mental health disorders in adolescents (Anderson et al., 2019), schools are the best avenue to implement theory-based intervention strategies with all students, so every child obtains optimal neurobiological brain development (Anderson & Teicher, 2008). It is a known fact that stressors and obstacles encountered (in school, society, or the environment) between the ages of 12- to 23-years-old can adversely affect the final brain maturation—creating aberrations in the brain (Selemon & Zecevic, 2015). Therefore, this is the crucial intervention window for adolescents who may be considered as clinically high risk for mental health symptoms (Velthorst et al., 2018).

- **Key Takeaways**

1. School-based intervention programs are known to increase the chances of identifying students with mental health diseases (Anderson et al., 2019).

2. Since everyone is affected by the pandemic, now is the perfect time to introduce and implement *The RGP* into schools—as an effective advisory or homeroom curriculum teaching tool.

3. With schools identified as ideal channels to help determine and assist at-risk students (Anderson et al., 2019), *The RGP* is one preventative method educators can utilize to help identify potential at-risk students.

4. The United States Department of Education has issued the following protocol to be implemented by district leaders in all schools that they "must prioritize addressing student mental health needs and utilize federal funding to provide professional development for educators on the topic of mental health" (United States Department of Education, 2022).

5. With this knowledge and the fact that we have all been affected by the pandemic, we can all benefit from utilizing *The RGP* which is broken into the following sections.

    - How *The RGP* Will Benefit Your Students and encourage a growth mindset
    - How Your Students Will Become Resilient Global Changemakers
    - How to Use *The RGP* where your student learners gain numerous cognitive, communication, and mindfulness life skills
    - What's Your Game Plan? Beginning with some "Warm-up" topics, followed by Topics addressing "Life Choices," "Life Crises," and "Relationships"
    - Additional sections: Notes, Appendix, Resources, Glossary of Terms, and References

• *The Resilience Game Plan* Pre-Assessment •

- **STEP #1:** Take this Pre-Assessment before moving forward with *The Resilience Game Plan*.
- **STEP #2:** Rank your Subjective Well-Being (from 1-10) and then *For every "Yes" response, write an "X" on the right-hand line.

Subjective Well-Being: (Rank from 1-10)

1. How satisfied are you with your life? (1 Extremely Unsatisfied - to - 10 Extremely Satisfied) _____
2. What are your feelings about people or situations in your life? (1 Extreme Anxiety - to - 10 Extremely Peaceful) _____
3. Do you feel your life has meaning and purpose? (1 Extremely Disagree - to - 10 Extremely Agree) _____

WHAT'S YOUR GAME PLAN? • WARM-UP

Academic Pressures:

1. Do you feel you belong and are connected at your school?
   - ☐ Yes - I belong to teams/clubs   ☐ No - I feel like an outsider   * (If "Yes," write "X" here:) _____
2. Do you find your schoolwork engaging and interesting?
   - ☐ Yes - I am learning for the "love of learning"   ☐ No - I am a "robo-learner"/only learn for tests   _____
3. Do you find your schoolwork meaningful and relevant to real life?
   - ☐ Yes - I am learning life-long skills   ☐ No - I am a "robo-learner"/only learn for tests   _____
4. Do you feel respected and valued at school?
   - ☐ Yes   ☐ No   _____
5. Do you have a close connection to at least one teacher at school?
   - ☐ Yes - list name: _____   ☐ No   _____

Habit Formation: New Habits and Breaking Old Habits:

1. Do you have habits you want to break? If Yes, list: _____ _____
2. Do you have new habits you want to form? If Yes, list: _____ _____

What's Your Legacy? Knowing Your Core Values:

1. How do you want to be remembered after you graduate? List: _____

Who Are Your Personal "Cheerleaders," Coaches, and/or Mentors:

1. Do you have a mentor/cheerleader in your life?
   - ☐ Yes - list name: _____   ☐ No   _____

WHAT'S YOUR GAME PLAN? • LIFE CHOICES

Self and Identity: List Your Peer Friend Group: _____

1. Do you associate your identity with your peer group? If "Yes," list your friend group on the line above and put "X" here: _____

Social Media:

1. Do you feel good about yourself after spending time on Social Media (e.g., Instragram, Snapchat, and TikTok)?
   - ☐ Yes - I feel good about myself.   ☐ No - I feel worse about myself   _____

Time Management - Life Balance:

1. Do you think you have a good life balance?
   - ☐ Yes   ☐ Average   ☐ No   _____

WHAT'S YOUR GAME PLAN? • LIFE CRISES

Abuse - Domestic, Physical, and Verbal:

1. Do you have a concern of feeling unsafe at school and home?
   ☐ Yes - List location: _____ ☐ No _____

2. Do you feel anxious at home (i.e., not enough food or do not feel protected)?
   ☐ Yes - List concern: _____ ☐ No _____

Anxiety:

1. Do you consider yourself an anxious person? If yes, list things that make you feel anxious:
   ☐ Yes - List: _____ ☐ No _____

Depression:

1. Do you feel depressed or down? If yes, list why you may feel this way or what makes you depressed:
   ☐ Yes - List: _____ ☐ No _____

Substance Abuse - Alcohol and Drugs:

1. Do either you, a friend, or a family member abuse alcohol and drugs?
   ☐ Yes - List: _____ ☐ No _____

Self-Harm:

1. Have you ever wanted to hurt yourself?
   ☐ Yes - List how you would hurt yourself: _____ ☐ No _____

WHAT'S YOUR GAME PLAN? • RELATIONSHIPS

Bullying/Cyberbullying:

1. Have you ever been bullied or been the recipient of cyberbullying?
   ☐ Yes - List situation: _____ ☐ No _____

Family or Guardian:

1. How would you rate your relationship with your family or guardian?
   ☐ Good   ☐ Average   ☐ Bad - List situation: _____

Friendship:

1. Are you in a peer-pressuring and/or non-supportive friend group?
   ☐ Yes - List your friends: _____ ☐ No _____

Peer Pressure:

1. Have you ever been put in a peer pressure situation?
   ☐ Yes - List situation: _____ ☐ No _____

List Your Stress Level Today (1 = not very stressed and 10 = very stressed)   **(1-10)** _____

© 2023 Reflections Publishing LLC. All rights reserved.
This book is sold with the understanding that the publisher and the author are not engaged in rendering medical, legal, or other professional advice or services.
If professional assistance is required, the services of a competent professional should be sought.

Section Two

Reflections Publishing Communication Assessment

(Page 9 in *The RGP: Student Edition*)

FOR LESSON PLANNING PURPOSES - 10 minutes total

- AMOUNT OF TIME TO ALLOCATE TO READ THE PLAYBOOK STRATEGY #3: LEARNING COMMUNICATION SKILLS: 6 minutes
- AMOUNT OF TIME TO ALLOCATE TO TAKE COMMUNICATION ASSESSMENT: 4 minutes

• It is recommended to have your learners read the Playbook Strategy #3: Learning Communication Skills section to educate themselves about the different "Preferred Methods of Communication." Your students can find this section on **pages 27-29** in *The RGP: Student Edition*.

*Student Edition Pages

Reflections Publishing Communication Assessment

Below, you will find questions to read and answer. The purpose of this assessment is to help you understand how your communication skills play a role and affect the way you communicate with others. For example, this questionnaire will show you why you might be struggling to communicate with a particular someone. If you pay attention to how an individual communicates with you, then you will likely find that this is their "Preferred Method of Communication"—meaning this is the best way to connect with them. Friends, family, fellow students, co-workers, neighbors, and group members can miscommunicate for years until someone in the relationship is willing to notice the disconnect and address the problem. Communication skills are valuable interpersonal tools for students to learn at a young age so they can use these skills during their academic years, when entering into personal relationships, and eventually navigating professional work environments.

Students can find more detailed information about each of the "Preferred Methods of Communication" on **pages 27-29**.

WHAT IS YOUR PREFERRED METHOD OF COMMUNICATION?

Choose One:
- ☐ Compliments and Praise
- ☐ Feeling Respected
- ☐ Friendliness and Caring
- ☐ Helping Hand
- ☐ Hugs
- ☐ Spending Time Together
- ☐ Token of Friendship/Gift-Giving
- ☐ Unconditional Love
- ☐ Other: _____

WHAT IS YOUR SECOND PREFERRED METHOD OF COMMUNICATION?

Choose One:
- ☐ Compliments and Praise
- ☐ Feeling Respected
- ☐ Friendliness and Caring
- ☐ Helping Hand
- ☐ Hugs
- ☐ Spending Time Together
- ☐ Token of Friendship/Gift-Giving
- ☐ Unconditional Love
- ☐ Other: _____

WHAT IS YOUR THIRD PREFERRED METHOD OF COMMUNICATION?

Choose One:
- ☐ Compliments and Praise
- ☐ Feeling Respected
- ☐ Friendliness and Caring
- ☐ Helping Hand
- ☐ Hugs
- ☐ Spending Time Together
- ☐ Token of Friendship/Gift-Giving
- ☐ Unconditional Love
- ☐ Other: _____

Additional Things to Think About:
- "Preferred Method of Electronic Communication?"
  ☐ Talking on Cell Phone ☐ Texting on Cell Phone ☐ Email ☐ Instagram ☐ SnapChat ☐ Other: _____
- Is your "Preferred Method of Communication" the same for your family and friends? _____
- Was there an event in your life that changed how you communicate with friends, family, coworkers, and schoolmates?
- Do you find it more difficult to communicate with people you are really close to or love? _____
- Do you have at least one person in your life that you can talk to when you are going through a tough time? _____

Ways to Improve Your Communication:
- Listen more than you talk, so you know what to discuss; try to separate issues, so things are not as overwhelming; be in sync with the person you are talking to and maintain an open mind; and keep emotions in check.

© 2023 Reflections Publishing LLC. All rights reserved.

Section Three

How *The Resilience Game Plan* Will Benefit You

•

Growth Mindset

(Page 11 in *The RGP: Student Edition*)

FOR LESSON PLANNING PURPOSES - AMOUNT OF TIME TO ALLOCATE TO READ THIS SECTION: 10 minutes
- 4114U pages on "How *The Resilience Game Plan* Will Benefit You" - 5 minutes
- Student Activity with Class or Group Discussion - 5 minutes

*Student Edition Pages

How *The Resilience Game Plan* Will Benefit You

Talking Points on Developing a Growth Mindset:

- By learning the tips and tools in *The Resilience Game Plan: The Playbook for Developing Cognitive, Communication, and Mindfulness Life Skills (The RGP)*, students will gain knowledge helping them to navigate difficult life scenarios. Nobody has a perfect life.

- Acknowledge to students that you did not "get the memo" that life is perfect—we all deal with something we are working to overcome as we progress through different chapters in our lives.

- The best way to tackle different situations throughout life is to develop a growth mindset.

- Encourage your students to develop a growth mindset now because they will benefit from this framework for the rest of their lives.

- A growth mindset is when you accomplish academic, personal, and work goals through hard work and determination. Evidence-based research conducted by Carol Dweck and others indicates the earlier you can create a foundation of a growth mindset along with positive and optimistic thinking, the sooner you are setting yourself up for a life of success and healthy emotional and social well-being.

- Encourage students to focus on their well-being during their adolescent years, as they are creating the foundation for their entire body from a cellular level. These are the cells that determine your physical and mental health, academic achievement, and even how you will socially adjust into society.

- Explain to students how acquiring habitual explanatory styles during their preteen and teenage years (such as a growth mindset and optimistic thinking) will impact their well-being for the rest of their lives. While these explanatory styles are likely influenced by a parent or guardian, they are also influenced by regular interactions with other significant adults in their life such as you, as well as a godparent, advisory or homeroom teacher, or coach.

- Researchers coined the concept of developmental resilience as they discovered that resilient children all seem to possess the following factors:

    1. Personal traits (e.g., compassionate to others, confidence in achieving goals, and intelligence)

    2. Responsive and supportive caregiver

- Share a personal story with your students about a time when you encountered life with a growth mindset. Next, share a time with them when you felt you had a fixed mindset (i.e., a time when you felt paralyzed when you did not succeed at something). Looking back, how in that same instance would having a growth mindset have propelled you from getting stuck.

- Encourage students it is okay to learn the material from you throughout the semester and miss some problems along the way. In some parts of the country, parents have their children take summer classes ahead of taking the same class at school.

- Emphasize to your student that they **have the ability to grow and develop into whoever they want to become. They can do anything they set their mind to, and their genetics and/or environment does not hinder them. While these variables can affect them, they do not have to define them.** It is through hard work, determination, attitude, experiences, and specific training that gives students brain power.

- **Share the advice from intelligence experts with your students:**

    1. Gilbert Gottlieb, a well-known neuroscientist, believes that your genes require input from your environment. Your genetics are not the only thing that determine your intelligence.

    2. Robert Sternber, who is known as an intelligence guru, would tell you that individuals considered experts are typically not people with a fixed mindset, but people engaged in the topic for a desired and specific purpose to learn.

    3. Alfred Binet would tell you that **the smartest children in the world in elementary school, do not always end up the smartest adults.** The reasoning is these children were likely raised with a fixed mindset—praised for their intelligence and not for the effort they took in learning the subject. These children also usually have a fear of failure. As an educator, you can identify these students when you see that something becomes hard for them or if upon receiving a bad grade, they become paralyzed in their learning process.

- **Tell your students why you think they should develop a growth mindset:**

    1. **Life is not always easy. We all have life challenges.**

    2. **Life is a marathon, not a sprint.**

- **When life gets hard, you need a game plan.**

    This where having a growth mindset and using the cognitive, communication, and mindfulness strategies listed in *The RGP* come into play.

    - Students are provided a safe space to download their feelings and tips and tools to help them navigate this post-pandemic world so they can live their best lives.

    - Student have a "How to Use *The RGP*" section that will walk them through how to get the most out of *The RGP*. This section explains how learning these intervention strategies will help them to navigate difficult emotions and life situations.

    - Remind your students that their parent(s) or guardian(s) are not going off to college with them or any other post-high school graduation plans they might have. This is now their time to make decisions. This is their life, not their parent's or friend's life. The anxieties of others and their past experiences do not need to influence your student's future. At the end of the day, they are the ones who will have to live with the consequences of their decisions.

- **Students now apply the concepts they read with these questions:**
  (Page 14 in *The RGP: Student Edition*)

1. Start with the first paragraph and number each paragraph in the outside margins. This allows you and your students to quickly reference paragraphs to discuss as a group.

2. In this section, every time students find the words **growth mindset**, circle the word in blue.

3. Have students write down their explanation regarding the benefit of developing a growth mindset versus having a fixed mindset.

_____
_____
_____

4. Have your students work in a small group and turn to the person they are sitting next to and exchange their definitions of a growth mindset:

_____
_____
_____

- **Notes:**

Section Four

How to Become a Resilient Global Changemaker

•

Character Development

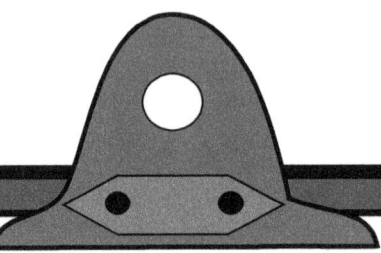

• Resilient Global Changemaker Game Plan •

The qualities below are discussed and integrated throughout *The Resilience Game Plan*. After your students complete this playbook, they will have increased their well-being and can check the boxes below for their newly gained skills:

- ☐ **Bridge Builder** who knows how to engage with community members and form intercultural relationships within communities on a local, regional, and global level.
- ☐ **Collaborative Visionary** who can gather, analyze, and synthesize information with a partner or in a group, then present data results, research, and innovative solutions.
- ☐ **Common Sense Mastermind** who is level-headed and smart, making good choices and behaving sensibly.
- ☐ **Community Service Leader** who exhibits prosocial behavior, is conscientious, reliable, relevant, and actively makes a positive impact to optimize human flourishing around the world.
- ☐ **Compassionate Trailblazer** who is caring, empathetic, happy, kind, and full of gratitude.
- ☐ **Confident Changemaker** who is balanced, engaging, charismatic, principled, and has high self-esteem and self-worth.
- ☐ **Critical Thinker** who explores different perspectives with "blue-sky thinking" and is analytical, inquisitive, open-minded, and an active participant in their learning process.
- ☐ **Global Citizen Contributor** who sees the big picture with an international perspective and is filled with dependability, forward-thinking, honesty, integrity, and social trust.
- ☐ **Growth Mindset Gamechanger** who has grit and resilience to overcome life difficulties.
- ☐ **Interpersonal Communicator** who is skilled in improving personal and professional relationships and is a constructive, effective, and respectful problem-solver.
- ☐ **Knowledgeable Analyst** who, in an unbiased manner, acknowledges any learning gaps, has an analytical nature of knowledge, and applies the Theory of Knowledge (TOK) concepts (e.g., Cultural, Empathy, Evidence, Explanation, Interpretation, Interconnectedness, Justification, Objectivity, Perspective, Responsibility, Truth, Values, and Visionary).
- ☐ **Lifelong Learner** who is curious and enjoys discovering real-life applications for materials learned across many curriculum subjects (e.g., languages).
- ☐ **Nature-Conscious Advocate** who implements a daily practice of sustainability and has a healing bidirectional relationship between humanity and our planet.
- ☐ **Risk-Taking Innovator** who is self-motivated, self-regulated, and forward-thinking.
- ☐ **Well-Being Connector** who is happy, healthy, and thriving due to their efforts and sense of belonging and social connection at school and within their community.

© 2024 Reflections Publishing LLC. All rights reserved.

Section Five

How to Use *The Resilience Game Plan*

(Page 17 in *The RGP: Student Edition*)

- Six Strategies for Success - 18
- Creating Your "Personalized Game Plan" - 18-19
- How to Use *The Resilience Game Plan* - 20-42

FOR LESSON PLANNING PURPOSES - AMOUNT OF TIME TO ALLOCATE TO READ THIS SECTION: 32 minutes

Instructions on How to Learn this Section:
- 4114U Life Topics - Read Page 20:   1 minute
- UNDERSTANDING BRAIN POWER - Read Page 20-21:   3 minutes
- LEARNING COGNITIVE SKILLS - Read Pages 22-26:   8 minutes
- LEARNING COMMUNICATION SKILLS - Read Pages 27-29:   5 minutes
- LEARNING MINDFULNESS SKILLS - Read Page 30:   2 minutes
- DEVELOPING NEW HABITS - Read Pages 31-41:   12 minutes
- REDUCING ANXIETY - GOAL SETTING - Read Page 42:   1 minute

---

*Student Edition Pages

• Six Strategies for Success •

Life happens, and when we hit bumps in the road, we all feel better knowing we have a game plan to navigate our lives through any difficult life scenario. When tough situations occur, you likely get upset or feel disappointed. You get to feel those emotions; however, the end goal is to always keep moving forward with a growth mindset and not get stuck in any situation.

In *The Resilience Game Plan (The RGP)*, when a difficult life situation hits, you are going to train your brain to:

1. **Acknowledge the life situation—processing any emotions.**
2. **Allow yourself to feel your emotions—describing your feelings of anxiety or distress.**
3. **Keep moving forward—applying the below steps to overcome your situation.**

• Creating Your "Personalized Game Plan" •

#1 In *The RGP*, you will incorporate these **three concepts** above into tackling any daily life situation and use the strategies below to create your "Personalized Game Plan."

#2 In *The RGP's* **"What's Your Game Plan" Sections Six-Nine**, you will find many different life topics. In order to successfully incorporate these concepts into your life, you need to learn these strategies and turn them into automatic habits. This game plan will train your brain to identify a situation and quickly process and move through any difficult life situation.

#3 Here is the game plan to become a **Resilient Global Changemaker** in any situation:

⇨ Read the two 4114U (**411**-Information **4**-for **U**-You) pages which will teach you about each life subject.
⇨ Complete the four activity pages to help you learn and process each specific life topic using the below strategies:
  • Strategy #1: Understanding Brain Power - See where and how this situation affects your brain
  • Strategy #2: Learning Cognitive Skills - Identify your thoughts, rate your feelings, and the steps to overcome your obstacle
  • Strategy #3: Learning Communication Skills - Gain interpersonal techniques to improve your relationships
  • Strategy #4: Learning Mindfulness Skills - Learn emotional self-regulation tools to help process your feelings
  • Strategy #5: Developing New Habits - Implement the "Well-Being Habit Tracker's" daily healthy habits
  • Strategy #6: Setting Goals and Reducing Anxiety - Set daily goals using the "Anxiety-Buster To-Do List"

• Six Pages to Create Your "Personalized Game Plan" •
Life happens—here's how you are going to work through it and move forward

4114U
2 pages to teach students about each life topic
Page 20

Strategy #1
Understanding Brain Power
Pages 20-21

Strategy #2
Learning Cognitive Skills
Step #1:
Expressive Writing Activity on
Pages 22-24

Strategy #3
Learning Communication Skills
and Activity on
Pages 27-29

Strategy #4
Learning Mindfulness Skills
Activity on
Page 30

Strategy #2
Cognitive Skills
Step #2:
Gauge Feelings Activity on
Page 25

Strategy #2
Learning Cognitive Skills
Step #3:
Overcoming Obstacles Activity on
Page 26

Strategy #5
Developing New Habits in the Habit Tracker
Activity on
Page 31-41

Strategy #6
Reducing Anxiety
Anxiety Buster To-Do List Activity on
Page 42

How to Use the Resilience Game Plan

-35-

• How to Use *The RGP* •

4114U [LIFE TOPIC] PAGES

Each life topic in *The RGP* will have **two 4114U pages** of informational pages before delving into four more pages of Brain Power, Cognitive, Communication, and Mindfulness Skills so students can create a game plan.

PLAYBOOK STRATEGY #1: UNDERSTANDING BRAIN POWER

In *The RGP: Student Edition*, Ster wrote in the "Introduction" that she wanted to bubble wrap their brains. She wants students to understand that the time period (between the early adolescent and young adulthood years) is a sensitive window of time when social and environmental stressors can potentially create a significant, negative impact —altering an adolescent's developing brain. Harvard scientists David Hubel and Torsten Wiesel named this brain process *plasticity*, when their brain is molded like plastic based on your life experiences.

In the book *Livewired,* neurologist David Eagleman takes the term brain *plasticity* (neuroplasticity) even one step further. He considers the human brain an "electric living fabric"—continually remolding itself with every life experience. He thinks the brain is a living organism, constantly rewiring itself based on every life situation a person experiences. Your good experiences and exposure to external stimuli create beneficial pathways in your brain, and bad experiences create aberrations (i.e. negative alterations) in your brain. Eagleman coined the phrase *livewire* in place of *plasticity* because the brain is constantly changing and the word *plasticity*, possibly meaning, occurring once and molded for good.

> **Key Takeaways**
> 1. Experiences early in life are significant in shaping brain development.
> 2. Evidenced-based research reports that neuroanatomical alterations are the cornerstone of experienced-based neural plasticity.
> 3. Any negative brain alterations that occur during adolescence need to be taken seriously, as this is the window of time to address these aberrations.
> 4. All environmental, social, and socio-economical experiences affect brain maturation where your higher-level cognitive functioning will continue to develop as you mature.

Therefore, as we move from each life topic in *The RGP*, students will use colored pencils to lightly color every "Key Takeaway" box in yellow (i.e., the color to get noticed). Also, they will color the part of the brain affected by the challenging life scenario. Go to **page 154 to see the Brain Power Color Chart** The reasoning behind having students color the part of the brain involved by each life topic is for them to fully understand the importance of where and why this particular life topic affects their brain. Plus, when students apply color to something, this is a good study strategy to implement because it helps them remember things.

Lobes of the Brain
- **FRONTAL LOBE:** voluntary movement, expressive language, planning, impulse control, and managing higher-level executive functions
- **OCCIPITAL LOBE:** vision (visual perception, identifying color, form, and motion)
- **PARIETAL LOBE:** movement and sensation (touch, taste, and temperature)
- **TEMPORAL LOBE:** language (processing auditory information and encoding of memory), emotion, and sexuality
- **CEREBELLUM:** coordination

• Human Brain Anatomy •

During your teenage years, your brain is only 80 percent developed—wiring together from the bottom up and from the back to the front. This explains why teens struggle with decision-making and making good choices, as the Frontal Lobe area is the last to develop. The synapses strengthen as brain cells in neural pathways and synapses are actively repeated. Thus, Shatz (1992) paraphrases the work of Donald Hebb (1949) that "what fires together, wires together."

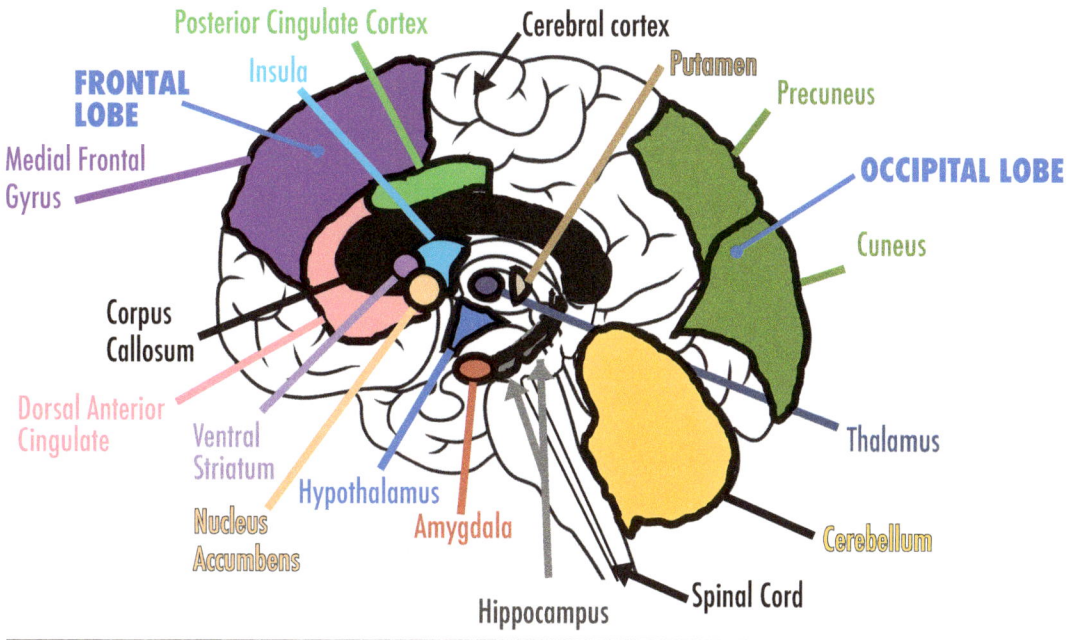

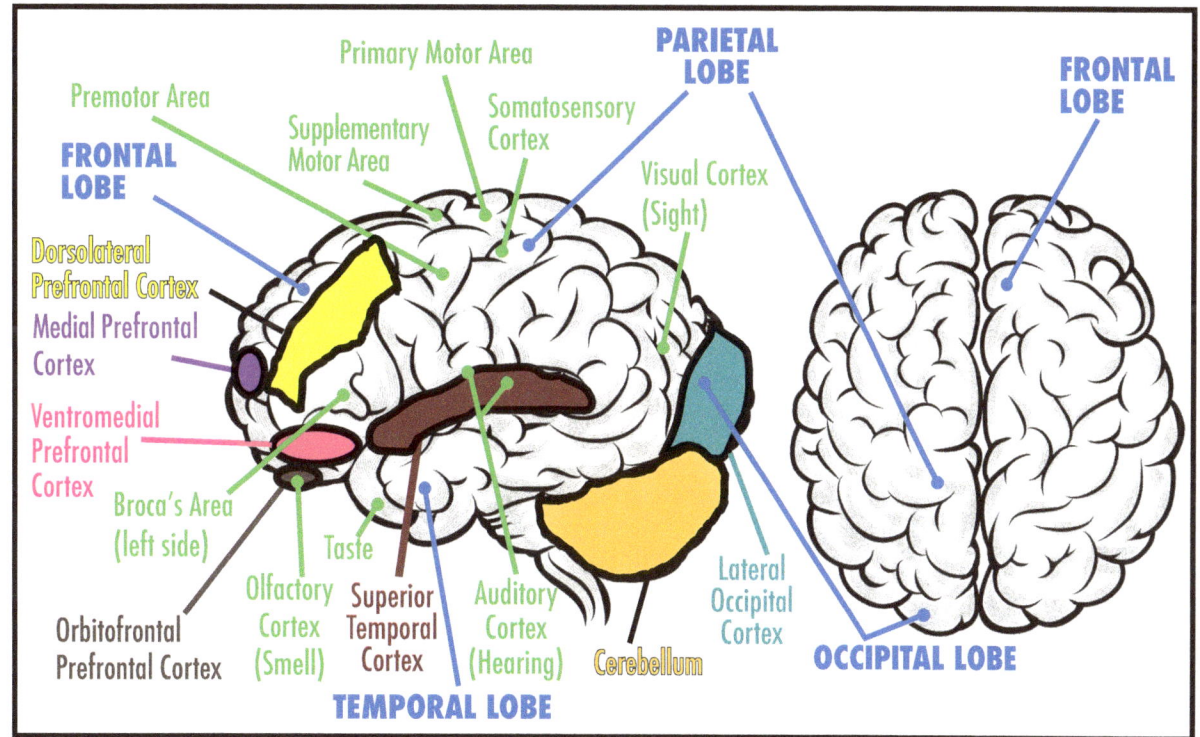

PLAYBOOK STRATEGY #2: LEARNING COGNITIVE SKILLS

Did you know that the average person has around 70,000 thoughts per day? Of those thoughts, 80 percent are negative, and 95 are repetitive. Unless we make a point to retrain our brains, negative thoughts will consume our lives. Cognitive Behavior Specialists have even created a term called Automatic Negative Thoughts (ANT), and nobody likes ants—critters or bad thoughts.

The good news is that evidence-based research supports the theory that we can all build new "brain pathways" and stop these negative and ruminating thoughts. Learning Cognitive and Communication Skills, along with mindfulness techniques, assist in creating these new brain pathways—giving students the tips and tools they need to have in their back pocket when needed most. These concepts include: determining personal values; setting goals; understanding emotions; identifying the cause of anxiety in the body; matching thoughts to feelings; recording thoughts, feelings, actions, and behaviors; and practicing mindfulness behaviors until they are habits. Also, the benefit of learning these Cognitive Skills techniques is that when adolescents feel depressed or anxious, *The RGP* strategies will teach them to automatically replace negative thoughts with more productive, positive, and beneficial cognitions.

The Cognitive Skills Training is divided into the following three steps:

Step #1: Expressive Writing

This section is a safe space for adolescents to process their feelings, thoughts, and any stress they might be experiencing. They are guided through this expressive writing exercise with four prompts:

#1 Stop and Acknowledge - What are you thinking/feeling?
This prompt encourages you to stop, catch, and acknowledge any anxious, fearful, negative, or stressful thoughts ruminating (i.e., repeatedly over and over) in your brain.

#2 Question and Tweak - What facts back up these thoughts?
Next, you want to question any negative or stressful thoughts and whether you have any evidence or facts to support why you are feeling a certain way.

#3 Balance and Thrive - I will change this negative thought in my head to this positive thought:
Then, put a stop sign up in your brain to halt the ruminating negative and stressful thinking and redirect and pave a new highway in your brain with a positive thought process.

#4 Create your "I Am Statement" in overcoming this obstacle:
Next, creating a powerful "I Am Statement" is an excellent way to practice a growth mindset through repetitive verbal affirmation with positive statements. Phrases such as "I am worthy" and "I am a hard worker" can build self-esteem and boost motivation. Additionally, creating an "I Am Statement" is a self-affirmation that can provide a barrier to harmful or threatening experiences, lower your feelings of stress, and improve your physical and mental well-being. Through "I Am Statements," these affirmations can elevate a student's academic performance. When you look through the lens of personally adopting a growth mindset, you are expanding your mind—academically, behaviorally, and emotionally.

"I Am Statements" are included in *The RGP* because these self-affirmations have potentially long-lasting effects as they can replace negative, ruminating thoughts by creating an adaptive, positive feedback loop in the self-related processing and reward pathways in the adolescent's brain.

Additionally, creating an "I Am Statement" is a self-affirmation that can provide students a barrier to harmful or threatening experiences, lower your feelings of stress, and improve your physical and mental well-being. Through "I Am Statements," these affirmations can elevate a student's academic performance. When you look through the lens of personally adopting a growth mindset, students are expanding your mind—academically, behaviorally, and emotionally.

"I Am Statements" are included in *The RGP* because these self-affirmations have potentially long-lasting effects as they can replace negative, ruminating thoughts by creating an adaptive, positive feedback loop in the self-related processing and reward pathways in an adolescent's brain.

Mechanism	Associated Brain Function Components
• Self-processing	Medial Prefrontal Cortex + Posterior Cingulate Cortex
• Valuation systems	Ventral Striatum + Ventromedial Prefrontal Cortex

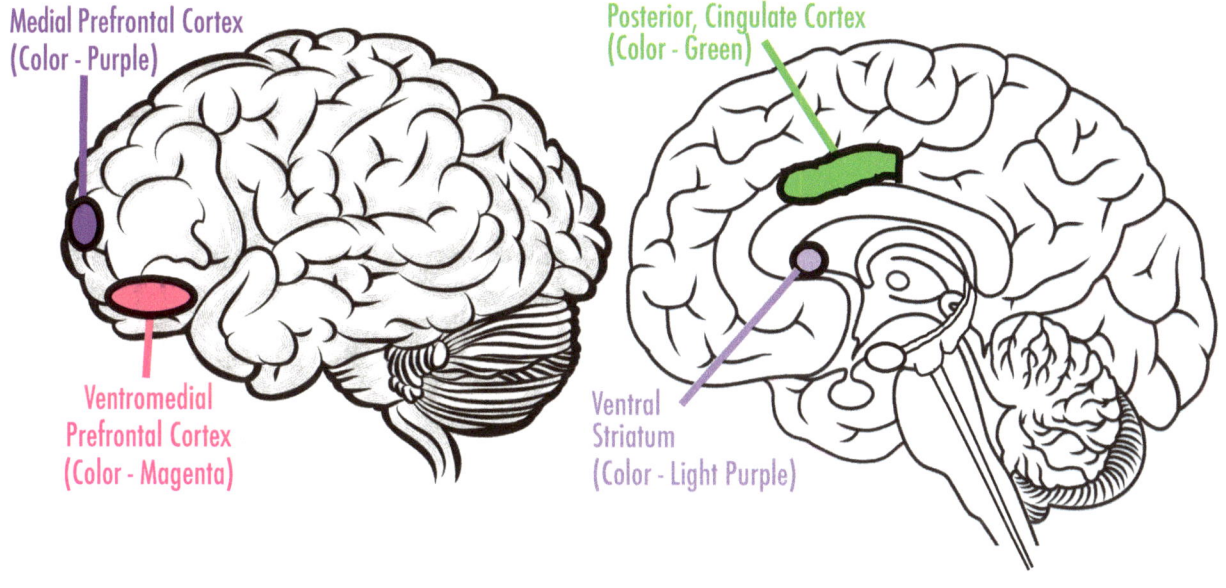

• Example of Step #1 - Expressive Writing to Overcome a Fear of Dogs

For training purposes, as students learn each of the three "**Cognitive Skills**" steps in *The RGP* playbook, they will use the life topic of **Overcoming a Fear** and example of how to **Overcome a Fear of Dogs**. This exercise gives adolescents and emerging adults permission to process their feelings and allows them to acknowledge the life situation they are working to overcome.

Middle School and High School Student Instructions:

This section is a safe space for students to process their feelings, thoughts, and any stress they might be experiencing. On the blank line, they will list the fear they are wanting to overcome. In this instance, the example is **overcoming a fear of dogs**.

Next, students are guided through this expressive writing exercise with four writing prompts:

Cognitive Skills   EXAMPLE

Step #1: Expressive Writing Activity to Overcome _a fear of dogs_

#1 Stop and Acknowledge - What are you thinking/feeling?
When I see a dog, I am afraid the dog is going to bite me. I feel like I am going pass out from the anxiety it causes me. I freak out whenever I see a dog, even when I know I will not come into contact with the dog.

#2 Question and Tweak - What facts back up these thoughts?
Why do I feel this way? I have never been bitten by a dog, so why do I assume a dog is going to bite me? My mom is afraid of dogs, so maybe that is why I am scared? I have no reason to be fearful of dogs.

#3 Balance and Thrive - Change your negative thought to this positive thought:
I want to change my scared and fearful thoughts about dogs to this positive thought: When I see a dog, it makes me smile and I feel happy; I am no longer afraid of dogs.

#4 Create your "I Am Statement" in overcoming this obstacle.
I am a courageous person that wants to try new things and become more adventurous.

After students work through the four writing prompts and have a better idea of how they are feeling, they will move on to **Step #2 - Gauging Your Feelings.**

Cognitive Skills

I want to overcome my fear of dogs.
(Write the "Fear" causing you distress that you want to overcome.)

• Example of Step #2 - Gauging Your Feelings

For training purposes, we will continue with the example of **Overcoming a Fear of Dogs**. Students will write on the above blank line the fear they are wanting to overcome. Next, they will gauge their feelings on the provided Subjective Units of Distress Scale (SUDS) "Feelings Thermometer." This is an excellent way to step back, acknowledge, and rate their level of anxiety/distress. To assist them in learning this new concept, they will find suggestions and ideas to help guide them to create their own list for each life topic in *The RGP* playbook. The goal is for them to learn how to assess their feelings and to always keep moving forward to overcome their obstacles. **(High schoolers will have a 10-unit scale, and middle schoolers will have a 5-unit scale, as seen below.)**

Middle School Student Instructions:
(High School Students will use a 10-unit scale.)

When students see the SUDS "Feelings Thermometer" illustration in each life topic section in *The RGP* playbook, they will:

- Use this gauge (to the right) to determine their SUDS rating. They will start at the bottom of this thermometer and list their feelings of anxiety/distress from 1 to 5. The bottom of this scale is marked in "units" with a coordinating line for them to **itemize their feelings from:**
  1. their least anxious and distressing thoughts
  up to
  2. their most anxious and distressing thoughts.

- Now, they should color their way up to the emotion they are feeling (between 1 to 5.)

- Once they determine their level of anxiety/distress, they should move straight to **Step #3** where they will create the necessary steps in their ladder to overcome their obstacle.

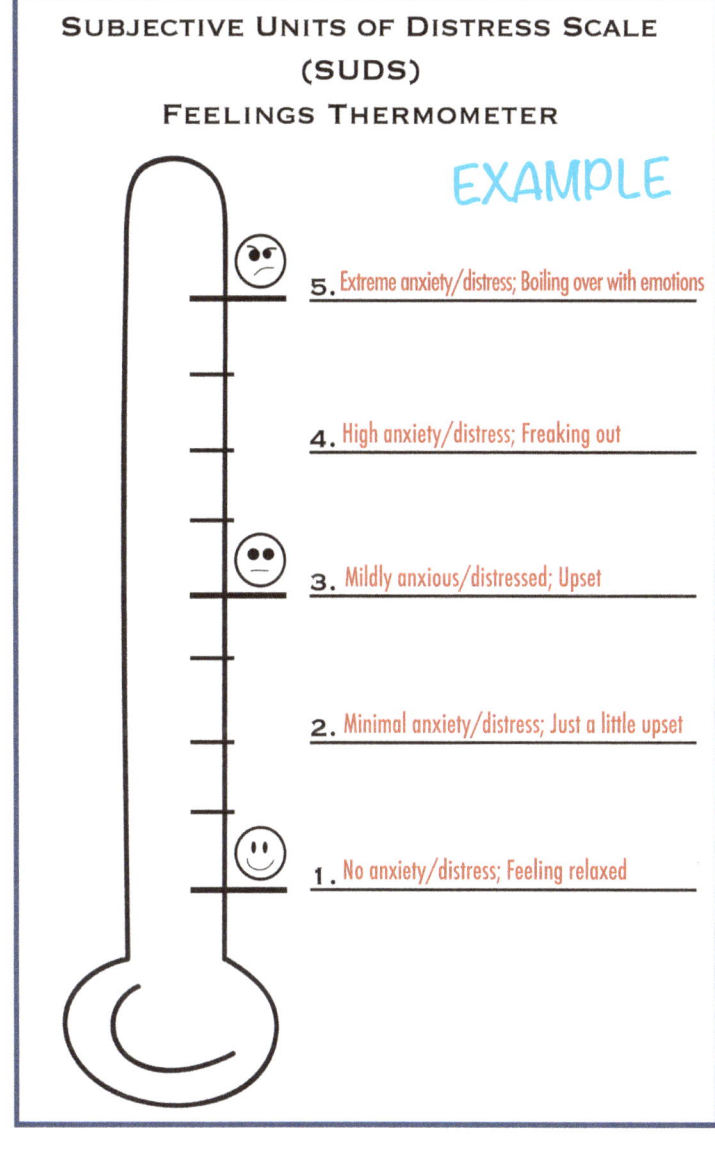

SUBJECTIVE UNITS OF DISTRESS SCALE (SUDS)
FEELINGS THERMOMETER

EXAMPLE

5. Extreme anxiety/distress; Boiling over with emotions
4. High anxiety/distress; Freaking out
3. Mildly anxious/distressed; Upset
2. Minimal anxiety/distress; Just a little upset
1. No anxiety/distress; Feeling relaxed

Cognitive Skills

I want to overcome my fear of dogs.

(Write the "Fear" causing you distress that you want to overcome.)

• Example of Step #3 - Overcoming Obstacles

Students have now completed **Step #2 - Gauging Your Feelings** to identify their anxiety and distress levels and SUDS rating. **Step #3** will keep them moving forward as they build their "Fear and Avoidance Hierarchy Ladder." This framework provides an exposure and response prevention (ERP) plan that identifies what will personally help them to work through their specific fears. As they build this framework, they must turn their focus inward as they self-assess what is triggering them and the baby steps they will need to take to overcome the situation.

Middle School and High School Student Instructions:

- Using the **Overcoming a Fear of Dogs** example, students will start at the bottom of the ladder (with their easiest exposure) and list their first baby step to overcome this obstacle. Step-by-step they will continue to build their ladder until they get to the top (with their most feared exposure.) At this point, they will have **overcome their fear of dogs** and **exposed themselves to ten different "feared" scenerios.** They will have succeeded in overcoming their obstacle.

- Students will quickly master this technique by repeatedly utilizing this strategy with any tough situation that comes their way. Life is not perfect, so the goal is to always be moving forward and use these coping skills to tackle any difficult life situation.

- Like **Step #2, Step #3** will also include suggestions and ideas, listed below the "Fear and Avoidance Hierarchy Ladder" illustraton for each life topic in *The RGP* playbook. A possible scenario is given for each life topic as an "idea starter" to help guide students to create their own list of exposures for the topic they choose.

EXAMPLE

FEAR AND AVOIDANCE HIERARCHY
WRITE EXPOSURES ON LADDER

10. Get a dog
9. Dog sit for a friend
8. Go to a dog park
7. Pet a dog off leash
6. Pet a dog on a leash
5. Hold a puppy
4. Go to a dog shelter
3. See a dog across the street
2. Watch TikToks about dogs
1. Look at a picture of a dog

PLAYBOOK STRATEGY #3: LEARNING COMMUNICATION SKILLS

Words are powerful and game-changing; learning communication skills at a young age can significantly improve and impact a person's interaction between family members, friends, neighbors, and coworkers. Utilizing *The RGP*, the goal is for your students to come away with new and strong communication skills.

When working with children, tweens, teens, and emerging adults, I always say **you do not have to be the smartest person in the room.** However, **you do need to have strong communication skills, common sense, a good attitude, be a hard worker (who is on time and present), and most importantly—always be kind and respectful.** Not having strong communication skills or knowing how to connect with people will tremendously impact your ability to reach your full potential.

Furthermore, just like we all learn in various ways, we communicate in different ways too. Back in 2008, working with my three daughters and my Girl Scout troop, Ster started a questionnaire to help identify ways that children and adults prefer to communicate and how their "Preferred Methods of Communication" can change over the years due to their environment and life events.

For students to discover their "Preferred Methods of Communication," they should go to page 10 to take the Reflections Publishing Communication Assessment. This questionnaire asks individuals of all ages to select their *Top Three* "Preferred Methods of Communication," which are listed in detail on the following *The RGP: Student Edition* on **pages 27-29**.

"Preferred Methods of Communication"

• Compliments and Praise

Everyone enjoys receiving praise, but for some individuals receiving praise is crucial to their personal development. One way to tell if somebody thrives with praise is if they are constantly giving you compliments. This is a tell-tale sign that this is the best way to communicate with this individual.

• Feeling Respected

When used as a noun, respect can mean when a person shows respect to another person or as a verb when you respect someone. Respect is also used in deference to an elder or to be polite; however, respect can run much deeper on a fundamental human level. True respect should lead us to oppose discrimination against other individuals (i.e., age, gender, sexuality, race or religion). Respect can stand for not silencing or insulting another human being—even if we fundamentally disagree with them. As an educator, you might find that your students just want you to respect them and take them seriously. Bottom line—when someone treats you in a way you would never consider treating them, it can be hard to process and feel respected.

• Friendliness and Caring

As television personality Mr. Rogers always said, "If you don't have anything nice to say, don't say anything at all." We all struggle with processing behaviors that are different from the way we personally operate; however, for people who consider caring/compassion, friendliness, and kindness at the top of their list, a bully or relational aggression is devastating to them. Plus, it takes much more energy to be mean than to be kind and mean people are typically just insecure. Inform your students that individuals who know their self-worth and identity do not generally put others down or bully people.

- **Helping Hand**

The best way to identify a person who prefers this "Method of Communication" is somebody who is always helping others. This person generally struggles to ask others for help and is used to doing things themselves.

When your students cultivate a civic responsibility at a young age, they lay a framework of compassion and sensitivity towards others. By learning compassionate skills at a young age, learners are preparing to be future problem solvers in our multifaceted, diverse, and complicated world. Emphasize to students that if they are volunteering to make sure they do it for the right reasons and not just to list on college applications.

- **Hugs**

The power of physical touch or a hug can fill a person's love tank. This same theory applies to people who desire a hug or physical touch as their primary way to show affection to others.

- **Spending Time Together**

As an educator, you might identify the importance of quality time with a student as one who is always coming to you for help. On a personal level, another way to pinpoint the necessity of quality time for a person is if they are always asking you to get together or planning the next get together.

Price (2008) noted in the American Time Use Survey that the quality of time between a parent and child decreases as a child gets older; these findings correlate birth order to a child's outcome. In a family with two children, research shows the first-born child receives 40 percent more time than the second-born child. If you know a student's birth order in their family, this may impact them needing your attention. Regardless, if quality time is crucial to a student, make sure you are fully present and give them your full attention.

- **Token of Friendship/Gift-Giving**

If a person is always giving you gifts, then this is a signal that gift-giving is an important form of communication to them. Even spending 24 hours a day/7 days a week with this individual will not fill their their emotional tank. In the classroom, handing out small reward tokens to this type of student is huge.

Note: Since close relationships are linked to an individual's sense of self, the gift giver may be motivated to purchase a gift they know their friend wants to receive; however, the gift giver can experience internal conflict when buying a gift that differs from their own personal identity and self-concept. Knowing and understanding the internal battle a purchaser experiences can explain how this can elevate a person's inner need to validate oneself with material items. This is also why a person whose "Preferred Method of Communication" is gifting will not fill their energy tank unless they are buying or receiving gifts.

- **Unconditional Love**

Some may question if unconditional love is actually a form of communication, but functional neuroimaging scans prove this as true. When comparing romantic versus maternal love in the brain, researchers discovered that by analyzing overlapping regions in the brain's reward system, this also proved unconditional love as a form of communication. Their findings showed a significant activation location in the experimental condition compared to the control condition. Also, Beauregard et. al., (2009) findings indicated that regions of the brain such as "the Middle Insula, Superior Parietal Lobule, Right Periaqueductal Gray, Right Globus Pallidus (Medial), Right Caudate Nucleus (Dorsal Head), Left Ventral Tegmental Area and Left Rostro-Dorsal Anterior Cingulate Cortex" all indicate that "unconditional love" is mediated by a distinct neural network relative to that mediating other emotions. This network contains cerebral structures known to be involved in romantic love or maternal love. Some of these structures represent key components of the brain's reward system.

- **Summary**

Identifying and recognizing a student, family member, friend, or coworker's preferred "Method of Communication" is the key to having successful relationships. When people know their communication strengths, it also helps them to identify their communication weaknesses. This assessment has shown we communicate better with people we do not know well. For those who experience this, the communication challenge is to learn how to best communicate with our close family and friends. When we feel hurt by family members, separating the anger and putting ourselves in a place to speak calmly is hard. Instead, we often push buttons to get even because we know that person so well we know exactly what will sting or strike a chord.

PLAYBOOK STRATEGY #4: LEARNING MINDFULNESS SKILLS

Mindfulness is a nonjudgmental awareness of experiences captured in the present moment that produces beneficial effects on an individual's physical and mental well-being. Hölzel et al. (2011) describe mindfulness meditation as having the ability to alleviate mental health and stress-related symptoms. Functional and structural neuroimaging studies have identified the below four neuroscientific mechanisms processes underlying these brain functioning components—working synergistically and enhancing self-regulation.

Mechanism	Associated Brain Function Components
1. Attention regulation	Anterior Cingulate Cortex (ACC)
2. Body awareness	Insula; Temporo-Parietal Junction
3a. Emotion regulation: reappraisal	Dorsolateral Prefrontal Cortex (PFC)
3b. Emotion regulation: exposure, extinction, and reconsolidation	Ventromedial Prefrontal Cortex; Hippocampus; Amygdala
4. Change in perspective on the self	Medial Prefrontal Cortex; Posterior Cingulate Cortex; Insula; Temporo-Parietal Junction

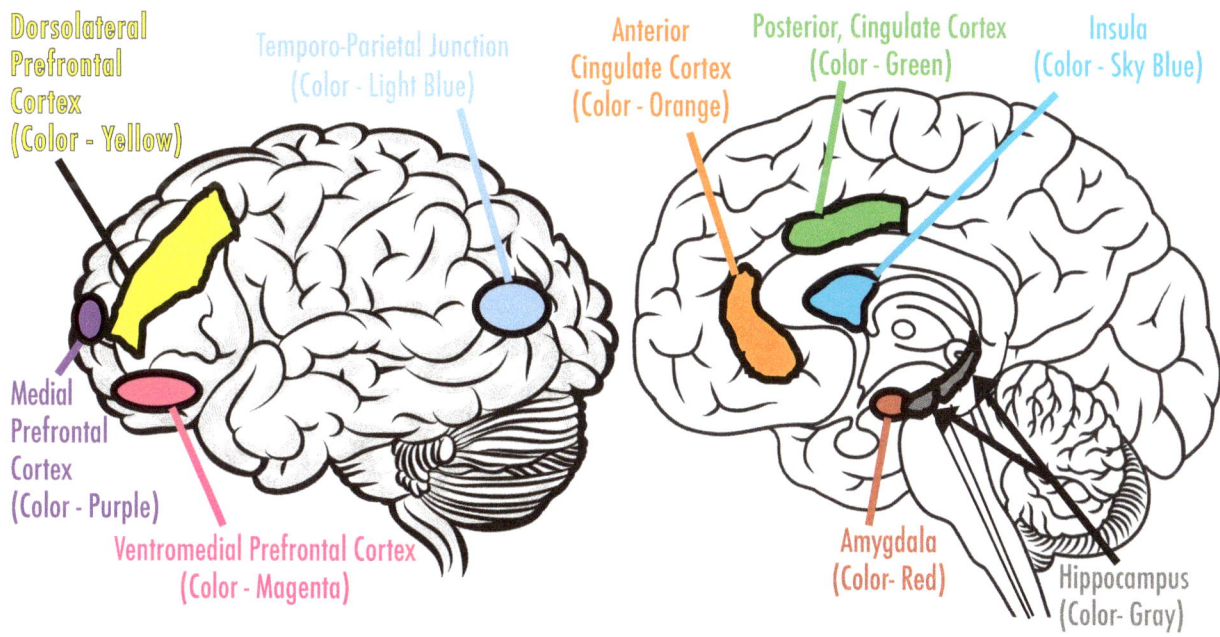

PLAYBOOK STRATEGY #5: DEVELOPING NEW HABITS

Students might find they are familiar with some of the concepts explained in *The RGP*. Incorporating some of these new habit-forming skills in their life might feel foreign to them— leading them to wonder:

- What exactly is a habit?
- How do you form a new habit?
- How do you break old habits?
- How long does it take to form a new habit?

Definition of Habit

In Julie Dirksen's book *Design How People Learn*, she defines a habit as "an acquired behavior pattern regularly followed until it becomes *almost involuntary*."

How to Form a New Habit

In *The RGP*, students are encouraged to keep an open mind and form some new habits; if they can develop a growth mindset, these habits will benefit them academically, behaviorally, mentally, and physically.

Dirksen divides the creation of new habit formation into six categories: ***an acquired behavior pattern, triggers, motivation, feedback, practice or repetition, and environment***.

#1 The **acquired behavior pattern** addresses the fact that we need to first learn the behavior before we can expect or want to make a new habit.

#2 According to B. J. Fogg, **triggers** are part of his behavior model:
Behavior = Motivation + Ability + Trigger

#3 Fogg maintains the theory that for a new habit to activate in your brain, this *almost involuntary* behavior must have a trigger that activates the new action or habit.

#4 Dirksen says for a habit to occur, the learner needs **motivation** and some control in the learning process.

The next component Dirksen lists is **feedback** which she acknowledges is an important part of creating a new habit. Dirksen also states that, unfortunately, very few new habits in the learning process have the luxury of immediate feedback.

#5 **Practice and repetition** are crucial in the learning process when developing new habits; habits become *almost involuntarily*. Dirksen expands on this concept stating when learning a new habit, this process is different for every person and the following four components come into play:

   i. Complexity and difficulty of a desired new habit
   ii. The mechanism that scaffolds and supports this new habit
   iii. The learner's motivation
   iv. The learner's feedback cycle

#6 The **environment** is the last category that Dirksen lists when forming a new habit. A learner is more likely to successfully implement a new habit in their life if they are in a supportive environment. For example, in *The RGP*, students are encouraged to get some form of exercise every day and find a workout partner or join a sports team —anything requiring accountability for the student to show up.

Utilizing these six ways to form new habits, in *The RGP*, students will find a section called **Well-Being Habit Tracker** which will encourage them to think through each of the following categories from the top category of **Exercise** to the bottom category of **Music**. Each category is discussed in detail, explaining why they are included in *The RGP* and why they should care about tracking this information.

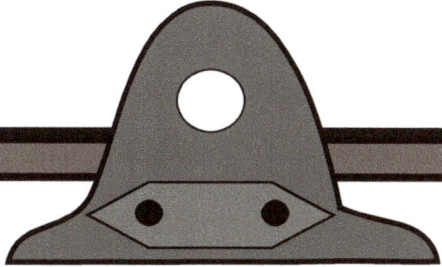

• Well-Being Game Plan •

The RGP "What's Your Game Plan" section will teach your students many new life skills. They are encouraged to turn these skills into automatic habits. In addition, in the **Well-Being Habit Tracker** below, students will find many daily habits to incorporate into their lives to help them achieve increased well-being.

From the moment students wake up, they should note the hours of **sleep** they get and, if possible, get outside for some **morning light exposure** to help set their circadian rhythm and start their day. The rest of the **Well-Being Habit Tracker categories** can be conducted throughout the day at their convenience while also noting their subjective well-being*.

Well-Being Habit Tracker: EXAMPLE

1. **Fill out each Well-Being Habit Tracker category below.**
2. **When completed, check the box and note your subjective well-being from 1-10.**

- ☐ **Sleep:** How many hours? _____ **Morning Light Exposure:** ☐   Well-Being Rating: ____
- ☐ **Exercise:** Length/Type? _____   Well-Being Rating: ____
- ☐ **Mindfulness:** Length/Type? _____   Well-Being Rating: ____
- ☐ **Nature:** Time spent/Activity outside? ____ / _____   Well-Being Rating: ____
- ☐ **Hydration:** I drank ☐☐☐☐☐☐☐☐ 8 oz. glasses of water.   Well-Being Rating: ____
- ☐ **Nutrition:** Number of healthy meals or calories consumed? _____   Well-Being Rating: ____
- ☐ **Social Fitness:** Time spent/Activity? ____ / _____   Well-Being Rating: ____
- ☐ **Caring:** Act(s) of service? _____   Well-Being Rating: ____
- ☐ **Gratitude:** I am grateful for _____   Well-Being Rating: ____
- ☐ **Happiness:** _____ brought me joy!   Well-Being Rating: ____
- ☐ **Laughter:** I laughed about _____
- ☐ **Smile:** I made someone smile by _____
- ☐ **Music:** I sang or listened to this song to motivate me and boost my mood and well-being: _____

© 2024 Reflections Publishing LLC. All rights reserved.

*   Subjective well-being is how you feel, your life satisfaction, and if you believe your life has meaning and purpose.
** Bright morning light is known to help you wake up and start your day.

WELL-BEING HABIT TRACKER

REFLECTIONS PUBLISHING LLC

Well-Being Habit Tracker Categories

• Sleep

Sleep is one of the most important things we do all day, and getting a good night's sleep is critical to a learner's health. Neuroscientist Dr. Frances E. Jensen states that **sleep is as important as the air you breathe and the food you eat, and it helps your students manage their stress levels.** Plus, research indicates a good night's sleep embeds everything learned that day into the student's working memory for them to access during a test. So students are encouraged to rest and not pull an all-nighter and get **at least 8 hours of sleep**.

Bright Morning Light. When you first wake up, expose yourself to bright morning light (e.g., sunlight or bright white light) to help you wake up and start your day. Many years ago, people lived outdoor lifestyles where sleep, moods, and circadian rhythmic cycles aligned with natural light cycles. For increased well-being, identify activities in nature during daylight hours to help your mood and sleep.

- **Exercise**

Physical activity (PA). Through evidence-based research, PA is strongly linked to well-being; PA is known to improve physical health which improves your neurocognitive health. PA as "any bodily movement produced by skeletal muscles that requires energy expenditure" and any activity that raises the heart rate above resting levels. Additionally, continued research in this area supports not only a positive relationship between PA and cognitive functions, but also academic achievement. When you get PA, your neurocognitive brain function is enhanced, specifically your executive functions (EF), which is a set of top-down mental processes that allows for controlled and goal-directed behavior.

Expert Adele Diamond subdivides executive functions into Three Core Dimensions:

- **First dimension: Updating** - how you maintain relevant information in working memory.
- **Second dimension: Inhibition** - when you avoid dominant, automatic, or proponent responses.
- **Third dimension: Shifting** - incorporates both updating and inhibition processes, along with the ability to transition between multiple tasks, operations, rules, or perspectives.

Animal and human studies analyzed the biological and psychological positive effects of PA on brain plasticity and epigenetic mechanisms. In regards to the psychological beneficial effects related to PA, the research shows significant benefits in a reduction of anxiety and depression when an ongoing and consistent training program is conducted (i.e., exercising over 30 minutes a day versus working out for a couple of days per week). After intense aerobic exercise (i.e., between 30 to 70 percent of maximal heart rate), a reduction in an individual's anxiety and depression is achieved. Even participating in an anaerobic activity, such as stretching, has a significant, positive impact on a person's mood.

Along with improved neurocognitive health, environmental psychology studies indicate that **getting outside every day and moving your body in a natural environment can provide psychological restoration**; as well as strong long-term health outcomes.

Key Takeaway

- Exercise 30 minutes every day with a consistent and ongoing training program or other planned activity.

Sweating/perspiring is how our body regulates its temperature and plays a role in preventing diseases. When you exercise, more sweat is needed to cool your body, and your muscles heat up. When you exercise for longer periods, work out more intensely, or work out in a hot environment (e.g., hot weather or hot yoga class), your sweat loss may cause a water/electrolyte imbalance in your body. Sweat consists of sodium, potassium, calcium, and magnesium, which are electrolytes; if you work out for long periods, you must replenish your body by drinking electrolytes (e.g., electrolyte hydration mix or sports drink). You want to continue to drink water throughout the day. If you have trouble drinking water, you can flavor your water with fruit infusions. You can also replenish your body with foods such as fruits (e.g., avocados, mangoes, pomegranates, and bananas), vegetables (e.g., green leafy vegetables and sweet potatoes), and legumes (e.g., chickpeas, kidney beans, and lentils), and calcium-rich foods (e.g., chicken, fish, milk, and yogurt).

In Persian medicine, sweating is considered to play an essential role in preventing and treating diseases. Sweating contains numerous health benefits (i.e., it removes waste products, maintains your body's health, and keeps your body temperature balanced).

• Mindfulness

Through mindfulness practice, individuals can cultivate a heightened focus on the present moment, leading to the development of positive qualities such as joy and compassion. This practice enhances attention, emotions, and behavioral self-regulation skills and improves overall well-being, making it a valuable addition to one's daily routine.

Christine O'Shaughnessy, who leads mindfulness meditation workshops at Harvard University, considers mindfulness a fitness routine to keep your brain healthy. Mindfulness keeps your mind on track by being aware when your mind wanders. Mindfulness is the power of your breath and connecting that breath to your body as you breathe in and out. O'Shaughnessy offers a mindfulness app called Present-Guided Meditation, which offers several free meditation sessions. Also, Harvard researchers discovered that practicing mindfulness 20 minutes a day will help you to be more focused, creative, productive, and less anxious.

In a CNBC interview, Lakhiani says, "For most people, 15 to 20 minutes will give you just the changes that you need. You can take a one- to three-minute dip into peacefulness and see remarkable results. The biggest benefits are going to happen in the first few minutes."

In a neuroscience-based mindfulness intervention program called Training for Awareness, Resilience, and Action (TARA), two different studies with 14- to 18-year-olds who participated in a 12-week group TARA training of mindfulness, yoga, and other therapy techniques showed significant improvements. In the smaller study, the depressed adolescents experienced decreased depressive and anxiety symptoms, along with improved sleep. In the other larger TARA study, the healthy control group reported increased emotional well-being, less anxiety, improved sleep quality, and positive changes within the inner white matter structural brain connectivity and outer gray matter volume.

Key Takeaways

- Research states that **20 minutes a day of meditation is optimal**; even 10 minutes a day delivers healthy brain benefits—which are seen in the first one to three minutes.

- As you practice mindfulness meditation with each life topic in *The Resilience Game Plan*, begin with the following steps before each recommended exercise:

    1. Find a quiet location to relax and either sit on the floor or in a chair.
    2. Align your spine by sitting up straight in a relaxed manner, with head and shoulders relaxed.
    3. Place your arms on each side, setting your hands face up on top of your legs.
    4. Now, close your eyes and start taking deep breaths to relax—noticing the power of your breath and connecting that breath to your body as you breathe in and breathe out.
    5. Since our minds like to wander, with no judgment, if you catch your mind wandering, return your focus to your breath.

- **Nature**

Dating back over two million years, our ancestors were entrenched in natural environments/outdoor therapy environments that helped them overcome challenges from abuse to toxic stress. These human survival experiences (i.e., having food, shelter, protection) are ingrained into our homo sapien minds still influencing brain functionalities in the present day; this therapy highlights the importance of our ancestor's outdoor lifestyle where sleep, moods, and circadian rhythmic cycles are aligned with natural light cycles.

The research supports the therapeutic values of human contact with nature assisting us with stressful and technology-driven lifestyles; moreover, evidence-based research supports the theory that **individuals can build "pathways" toward comprehensive health benefits**. Environmental psychology research studies provide hope that when individuals are immersed in a natural environment, it can provide **psychological restoration**. Spending at least 120 minutes a week in nature is associated with positive correlations for both health and well-being. Encourage your learners to develop a strong connection to nature so they will experience an improved physical and mental (i.e., reduced anxiety, depression, and stress) well-being.

Additionally, students should identify some hobbies and/or outlets in nature during hours with sunlight, and they will find that their mood is improved and they will have a better quality night's sleep. Lastly, nature therapy studies have shown decreased heart rates after participants viewed nature scenes compared to pre-test and post-test assessments of videos of natural and urban environments.

For example, in a study by Kim et al. (2010), if a 14-year-old is given a routine brain scan (as found in data collected in fMRI studies when individuals see images of a scenic natural environment), these testing maneuvers can determine if the adolescent also experienced increased brain activity in their Anterior Cingulate Gyrus, Globus Pallidus, Putamen, and head of the Caudate Nucleus areas. The importance of these findings is encouraging because it means that simply spending time out in nature or getting outside shows an increase in these brain areas, which are linked to one's positive mental, physical, and emotional well-being.

> **Key Takeaway**
>
> - Spending at least 120 minutes a week in nature or outside is associated with positive correlations for both health and mental well-being.

Grounding. When using *The RGP*, if possible, go outside and take advantage of the natural healing power of the earth and place your bare feet on the concrete, dirt, grass, gravel, or wet sand. A study published in the *European Biology and Bioelectromagnetics Journal*, discovered that if you get grounded every day, it will calm your busy mind and reduce stress and tension. It shifts your nervous system from a stress-stimulated sympathetic mode to a calmer parasympathetic mode. Research by Oschman states grounding (earthing) provides a safe therapy that can help to optimize and balance your unique physiological functions. Oschman reports that if you think of your body as a continuous semiconducting fabric, when you ground it, this negative charge permeates into every part of your body (i.e., interiors of the cell and its nuclei). Thus when these mobile electrons are grounded, they quickly neutralize any free radicals in your body.

Mousa (2022) states it is contact with the earth via several channels that can cause an influx of electrons into your body, producing anti-inflammatory effects, immunity enhancement, anticoagulation, rising blood oxygenation, and antipyretic effects. Mousa also states that while any time spent "getting grounded" is excellent, the optimal amount of time to achieve your ultimate health is grounding for at least 40 minutes daily. Also, Mousa (2016) produced findings that individuals who spent time "getting grounded" showed symptomatic improvement in chronic muscle and joint pain, a reduction in overall stress levels and tensions, and a boost in positive moods.

Key Takeaways

- Get "grounded" for at least 40 minutes a day.
- Students have been provided with a good excuse regarding why they need to go to the beach or park.

• Hydration

The goal is to drink a minimum of eight 64-ounces glasses of water daily (Wong et al., 2017). Our bodies are comprised of 60% water, so it just makes common sense that if we sweat every day, we would need to replenish our bodies with water. Mousa (2022) states the concept of "getting grounded" with drinking water helps to excrete toxins from our body. Research also reports that a drink red in color can encourage us to drink more, as well as also increase our mood and cognitive abilities.

Maintaining hydration is significantly associated with a person's excellent physical condition and cognitive performance. With the brain comprised of 70% water (compared to 60% in the human body), staying hydrated is essential, as an adequately hydrated brain is known via brain imaging to improve mood, enhance memory, and decrease anxiety symptoms. Even with a body weight loss of 0.72%, drinking water improved memory and attention while reducing anxiety. With dehydration, you lose less than two percent of your body weight— negatively affecting a person's mental and physical state; recent research indicates that even a body mass loss of 0.55% is linked to increased anxiety, and a 0.66% body mass reduction creates disrupted functioning.

Key Takeaway

- The goal is to drink at least eight 64-ounce glasses of water daily. Ask your doctor for the recommended amount for your age, how much you exercise, and whether you live in a warm climate.

- A drink red in color will increase your mood, cognitive abilities, and your desire to drink more fluid Add a touch of cherry, cranberry, or pomegranate natural juice to your water.

• Nutrition

In one sentence, the summation of this category is—**you are what you eat**. In a meta-analysis of 12 fMRI case studies by Olivo, Gaudio, & Schiöth (2019), when adolescents do not eat a proper nutritious diet, then cognition is impaired, working memory is compromised, and social cues and empathy are lacking—causing an increased higher-level of anxiety, and poorly altered perspective-taking abilities. As your body grows, focus on eating a whole-food diet rich in vitamins and nutrients.

In the *Appendix* on **page 153**, students will find a **Nutrition Game Plan**. They can make copies of that page or start a daily food log on their computer or in a "Notes" section on their cell phone. Keeping track of what time of day they eat; where they eat; how they feel/think when eating; exactly what foods they are eating; and keeping track of their daily calories consumed will help them not to overeat and also keep track of the foods that make them feel good and/or bad.

• Social Fitness

In addition to maintaining our physical fitness, we must also invest in our social fitness. In a Harvard study conducted over eight decades by Waldinger & Schulz (2023) entitled *The Good Life* can be summarized into eight words and two sentences:

"Good relationships keep us healthier and happier. Period."

Furthermore, Waldinger & Schulz (2023) discuss several longitudinal studies that also report significant findings on the importance of human connections; these studies report that if people live lonely lives, they also have a shorter life expectancy (Seewer et al., 2022). In fact, Great Britain is addressing this public health concern in their country by appointing a Minister of Loneliness.

Umberson & Mortez (2010) expand on this thought process that the social relationships in your life have short- and long-term impacts on your physical and mental health. They also state that the social skills you develop during childhood have a cumulative effect progressing into adulthood.

Layard (2020) connects many concepts, life skills, and strategies in *The Resilience Game Plan*. In the **Well-Being Habit Tracker,** Layard encourages you to practice your "Social Fitness" and prosocial behavior—accomplished by showing empathy, compassion, and "Caring" through acts of service. As Layard supports with his research, for you to experience happiness, you need to practice your "Social Fitness" by spending time with family and friends, getting involved in social activities, and having a sense of belonging in your school and community.

• Caring

As mentioned in the **"Preferred Method of Communication - Helping Hand"** section, it is important to learn the life skills of being a caring, compassionate, empathetic, respectful, and sensitive person so we can make a positive difference to those in our community and around the world. By taking on this global civic responsibility framework, you become a community service leader who is conscientious, reliable, relevant, and always actively making a positive impact within communities worldwide. You exhibit prosocial behavior (compassion and social trust) and perform acts of service, such as exhibiting the daily practice of sustainability (composting and picking up trash) to collecting hygiene kit items to pass out to the homeless population.

• Gratitude

Gratitude is an emotion and attribute that, when practiced daily, is strongly correlated to your overall health and well-being. Incorporating the daily practice of gratitude helps students to open their eyes to all of the positive aspects of their life that they may not stop to appreciate until they write them down in their **Well-Being Habit Tracker**. To help learners to get started, here are some questions to assist them in their daily practice:

- **Awe and Wonder** - What causes you to stop and pause in awe to appreciate a certain beauty?
- **Thankfulness** - Identify the aspects and people in your life where you feel thankful.
- **Verbalize Your Appreciation** - Write down phrases you say to others to express your thanks.
- **Life is Short** - List the positive experiences in your life, along with future bucket list items.

When learner's practice gratitude daily, they are paving the neural pathways in their brain to make it an automatic habit to recognize all of the positive aspects in their lives. In a study with teenagers and young adults, MRI imaging captured the practice of gratitude journaling in the ventromedial prefrontal cortex and nucleus accumbens areas, considered "value-sensitive" and reward systems cortical brain regions. Researchers discovered these brain changes lead to more prosocial behaviors and moral emotions known to increase your well-being.

• Happiness

According to the **University of Oxford's Wellbeing Research Centre's World Happiness Report,** several factors influence our happiness and well-being. In this report, Oxford researchers analyzed the results of children, adolescents, and young people in these subjective well-being domains:

- **Life Satisfaction** - How happy or satisfied are you with your life?
- **Affect** - What are your feelings, emotions, and state of mind, positive (joy and happiness) and negative (sad and anxious), regarding people or situations in your life?
- **Eumaimonia** - Do you feel your life has purpose and meaning?

Encourage your students to become skilled and trust themselves to self-assess their well-being. They are reliable and capable of addressing these questions. Their well-being now affects their happiness into adulthood and their desire to obtain a higher education, which can lead to a better job and increased income.

Also, when learners identify leisure activities and outlets at their age, it is vital in assisting them to lead a well-balanced and wholesome life. Make sure they discover some active leisure activities such as physical and social activity, volunteering/acts of community service, and outdoor activities, are also important in increasing their overall happiness and well-being.

- **Laugh**

    Laughter is a known thing to have physiological, psychological, social, spiritual, and quality-of-life benefits. In contrast, as found in other areas of medicine, no adverse effects are known. The therapeutic efficacy of laughter is typically induced by external stimuli (i.e., a display of positive emotion, or self-induced laughter). Since the brain cannot distinguish between internal versus external stimuli, similar benefits are assumed to be achieved with both factors. **Researchers continue to monitor laughter as a healing agent since it possesses many positive and quantifiable effects on an individual's health**. In the **Well-Being Habit Tracker,** learners are asked to name something that makes them laugh each day, as well as list a way they made someone smile.

- **Smile**

    Theory and research indicate that individuals with more frequent positive emotions are better at attaining goals at work and have better mental health, physical health, and longevity (Abel & Krueger, 2010). Even fifty years later, research still supports these facts claimed by Izard (1971), stating that positive and negative emotions significantly correlate with an individual's personality and life outcome—influencing how that person will act, think, react, and interact with others.

- **Music**

    Going back to the prehistoric era, music has always played a vital role in expressing emotion (i.e., compassion and fear), as well as serving relaxation and healing purposes. Hippocrates, the founding father of rational medicine, and Plato are known to utilize music to soothe patients. Furthermore, going back to 870 CE, the Persian philosopher, Farbi also stated that music promotes good moods and emotional steadiness.

    A learned, cognitive response validates the effectiveness of music; the associated learning process can get rooted in your memory. Additionally, research states that **music increases dopamine and serotonin levels in the brain**. Listening to music is known to reach a cellular and epigenetic level in the human body—regulating human microRNA expression. So students are encouraged to get their groove on in the **Well-Being Habit Tracker** and list a song that lifts their spirits and motivates them to overcome any challenging situation.

PLAYBOOK STRATEGY #6: SETTING GOALS AND REDUCING ANXIETY

This sixth strategy of "Setting Goals and Reducing Anxiety" piggybacks perfectly to the previous five strategies the students just learned. Below is the formula learners need to create an overall healthy well-being of mind and body.

> **Learn Cognitive, Commununication, and Mindfulness Life Skills (Make Automatic Habits)**
> **+ Implement the Well-Being Habit Tracker Categories (Make Automatic Habits)**
> **+ Set Goals to Reduce Anxiety in Anxiety-Buster To-Do List (Make this an Automatic Habit)**
> **= Healthy Well-Being of Mind and Body**

While this **Anxiety-Buster To-Do List** exercise can be used on a daily basis, for the purposes of *The RGP*, you will see this **Anxiety-Buster To-Do List** chart at the end of every *RGP* life topic as you create your "Personalized Game Plan" for that particular topic. By using this **Anxiety-Buster To-Do List**, you will increase your ability to accomplish your goals and timely complete your tasks by listing out: **1 Big Task, 2 Medium Tasks, and 3 Small Tasks**.

According to Masicampo & Baumeister (2011), when you outline or create a list of your goals, you will experience the following:

- Several psychological benefits (i.e., reduces anxiety and keeps focus on success)
- As research indicates from the Zeigarnik Effect, unfinished goals will not deter you from interrupting thoughts, as unaccomplished goals are just distracting.
- When you create and commit to your game plan, it will open up your mind to other pursuits—allowing you to be more creative too.

Anxiety-Buster To-Do List: *EXAMPLE*

1 Big Task - Let's Go!

☐ _____

2 Medium Tasks - Let's Do This.

☐ _____
☐ _____

3 Small Tasks - You Got This.

☐ _____
☐ _____
☐ _____

© 2024 Reflections Publishing LLC. All rights reserved.

Section Six

What's Your Game Plan?

Warm-up

(Page 43 in *The RGP: Student Edition*)

LIFE TOPICS:

- Academic Pressures - 44
- Habit Formation: Forming New Habits and Breaking Old Habits - 50
- What is Your Legacy? - Core Values - 56
- Who are Your Mentors/Coaches? - 62

*Student Edition Pages

• Academic Pressures •

> **FOR LESSON PLANNING PURPOSES - AMOUNT OF TIME TO ALLOCATE: 26 minutes**
> *Add 4 minutes to take the Reflections Publishing Communication Assessment/Add time to the Mindfulness section (if possible), as 20 minutes provides optimal benefits.
>
> - 4114U and Student Activity - 5 minutes PLUS Class Discussion - 7 minutes
> - Playbook Strategy #1: Understanding Brain Power - 1 minute
> - Playbook Strategy #2: Learning Cognitive Strategies - 10 minutes
>   - Step #1 Expressive Writing - 2 minutes
>   - Step #2 Gauging Your Feelings - 4 minutes
>   - Step #3 Overcoming Obstacles - 4 minutes
> - Playbook Strategy #3: Learning Communication Strategies - 1 minute
>   - *Reflections Publishing Communication Assessment - 4 minutes
> - Playbook Strategy #4: Learning Mindfulness Strategies - 4 minutes
> - Playbook Strategy #5: Developing New Habits - 2 minutes
> - Playbook Strategy #6: Anxiety-Buster To-Do List - 1 minute

• Facilitator Talking Points: (Page 44 in *The RGP: Student Edition*)

1. With a growth mindset, you can achieve success in any major if you are passionate and work hard at it.
2. Stanford's Challenge Success Program is a school and community-based intervention program that supports students by reducing the pressure cooker mentality—getting back to the love of learning.
3. Sometimes, adults unnecessarily pass their fears or try to live vicariously through children.
4. Tell your students that if they are struggling in school and feel like they need some additional help, to come talk to you. Maybe the reason the student is struggling is due to an undiagnosed learning disability.
5. Remind your students that none of us are perfect or born perfect, so if they feel like they are struggling in school or spending a long time completing their work, they should come talk to you.
6. Your students' brains are like plastic and can build new brain highways—no different than practicing to hit the right music note or learning the proper sports technique to hit the game-winning shot—it all takes practice. Everyone learns things differently.
7. Encourage your students to speak up if they are experiencing or living in a stressful situation, as this will affect their concentration and academic performance.

• Discuss Study Tips:
(The following suggestions are possible examples based on your students' living environment.)

1. Before studying, find a healthy snack to give them a boost of energy/maintain blood sugar levels.
2. Find a quiet place to study—with no distractions.
3. When taking notes, writing in red and blue colors can enhance students' cognitive skills (e.g., concentration and attention span) while also increasing their brain function (i.e., learning new information while embedding it into their working memory to encode, store, and retrieve this new information). The color red is known to enhance their performance on simple, detail-oriented tasks; in contrast, blue improves performance on simple and difficult, detail-oriented tasks, and on creative tasks.
4. Implement Repeated Reading (RR), which is a reading strategy that can improve their reading.
5. Free voluntary reading can increase their ability to read, write, spell, and comprehend.

• Academic Pressures Student Activity: (Page 45 in *The RGP: Student Edition*)

Have your students take some time to write down some ideas on ways they can destress and implement some of the study techniques they just learned.

Brain Power (Page 46 in *The RGP: Student Edition*)

When students are actively learning, they get a huge dopamine blast in their brain when they are learning for the love of learning. The main idea to emphasize to students is that if they are a student who is constantly stressed, research indicates they may experience a shift in their **Hypothalamic-pituitary-adrenal (HPA) axis** reactivity. Thus, this creates a perfect storm in their brain—resulting in a heightened stress-induced hormonal response. We all have a fight or flight response to help protect us in threatening situations; this cortisol release is a good thing to elevate their ability to respond to a potential threat. However, when a continual cortisol release occurs in their brain due to ongoing stress, this deactivates the **Hippocampal** brain region corresponding to heightened cortisol release. Too much cortisol in the brain is toxic. The mindfulness section in *The RGP* will be excellent in helping students to cope with their stress and lower their cortisol levels.

As an activity, you can have your students type HPA axis stress response system in their web browser to see the entire HPA cycle from the **Hypothalamus** → Pituitary Gland → Adrenal Gland

When the HPA axis stress response system is overly activated, it affects the immune system with the surge of cortisol released → which then swings back up to the **Hypothalamus**.

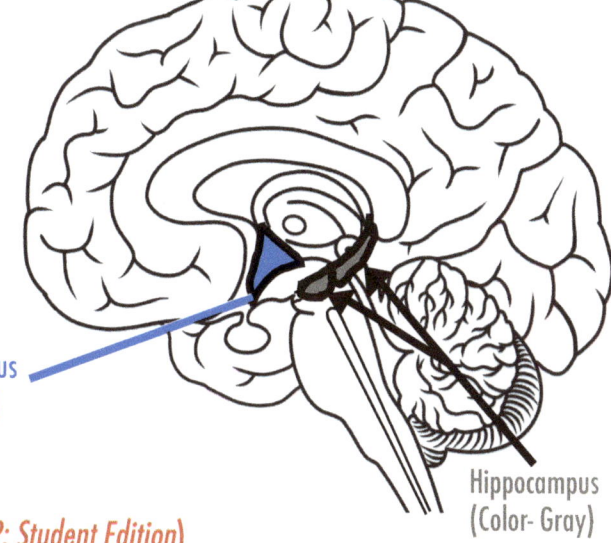

Hypothalamus (Color- Blue)

Hippocampus (Color- Gray)

Cognitive Skills (Page 47 in *The RGP: Student Edition*)

• **Talking Points for Cognitive Skills Section:**

Step #2: Gauging Your Feelings

How you Might Feel About Taking Tests:

10. Extreme anxiety/I feel like I'm having a panic attack.
9. Very anxious/My heart is racing.
8. High anxiety/I feel like I studied the wrong material.
7. Moderate-to-high anxiety/I feel overwhelmed.
6. Moderately anxious/I don't feel like I studied enough.
5. Mild-to-moderate anxiety/I feel okay going into this test.
4. Mild anxiety/I think I read and studied the right material.
3. Minimal anxiety/I feel like I am in a study groove.
2. Feeling good/I feel like I am concentrating well.
1. No anxiety/I feel confident in my study skills.

Step #3: Overcoming Obstacles

Ideas on "Overcoming Fear of Tests"

10. I am confident to take this test.
9. I will take the practice test to prepare.
8. I will create my own practice test to prepare.
7. I will do the breathing exercise that helps me to relax.
6. I will practice "I am" statements to increase my confidence.
5. I will work with a tutor to help with those hard concepts.
4. I will join a study group and identify what I still need to learn.
3. I will watch online videos with lessons about my test.
2. I will watch a movie about students taking tests.
1. I will listen to an upbeat song about overcoming a fear.

If any information in this playbook is upsetting, please talk to a parent/guardian, school counselor, teacher, or medical professional.

This book is sold with the understanding that the publisher and the author are not engaged in rendering medical, legal, or other professional advice or services. If professional assistance is required, the services of a competent professional should be sought.

• Habit Formation •

> **FOR LESSON PLANNING PURPOSES - AMOUNT OF TIME TO ALLOCATE: 25 minutes**
> *Add 4 minutes to take the Reflections Publishing Communication Assessment/Add time to the Mindfulness section (if possible), as 20 minutes provides optimal benefits.
> - 4114U and Student Activity - 6 minutes PLUS Class Discussion - 8 minutes
> - Playbook Strategy #1: Understanding Brain Power - 1 minute
> - Playbook Strategy #2: Learning Cognitive Strategies - 10 minutes
>   - Step #1 Expressive Writing - 2 minutes
>   - Step #2: Gauging Your Feelings - 4 minutes
>   - Step #3 Overcoming Obstacles - 4 minutes
> - Playbook Strategy #3: Learning Communication Strategies - 1 minute
>   - *Reflections Publishing Communication Assessment - 4 minutes
> - Playbook Strategy #4: Learning Mindfulness Strategies - 2 minutes
> - Playbook Strategy #5: Developing New Habits - 2 minutes
> - Playbook Strategy #6: Anxiety-Buster To-Do List - 1 minute

• Facilitator Talking Points: (Page 50 in *The RGP: Student Edition*)

1. In the *Design How People Learn book* by Julie Dirksen, she defines a habit as "an acquired behavior pattern regularly followed until it has become *almost involuntary.*"

2. **On pages 31-32**, Dirksen breaks down the creation of habit formation into six categories: **an acquired behavior pattern, triggers, motivations, feedback, practice or repetition, and environment.**

3. According to Chip and Dan Heath in their book *Switch*, as well as B. J. Fogg's Tiny Habits program, if you are feeling overwhelmed with acquiring a new habit, then name and identify the smallest productive behavior task and make the task feel smaller and more manageable.

4. **Breaking Old Habits:** Author James Clear in *Atomic Habits: An Easy & Proven Way to Build New Ones & Break Bad Ones* describes learning new habits as a gradual process. Clear states if you are struggling to change a habit, it is likely "your "system," and you have the wrong "system" for change, thus not achieving your goals. Strategies to make new habits include overcoming a lack of motivation and willpower, designing your environment to ensure success, and getting back on track when you fall off course.

   Clear uses a sports analogy that, as a coach, your goal is to win the championship. The "systems" are the processes you implement to recruit players, manage your coaching staff, and facilitate practice. Constantly tweaking and improving your "systems" is the best framework, and every effort toward forming a new habit builds like "compound interest"—even a one percent improvement adds up in the long term.

• Three Layers of Behavior Change Student Activity: (Page 51 in *The RGP: Student Edition*)

Students are given the following activity with an illustration of a dartboard on how to break an old habit.

1. **Outcomes** are the first and outer layer in achieving behavioral change. For example, this is a desire to get homework done quicker. **Color - Blue**

2. **Processing** is the second and middle layer. Students write out steps to help them get homework done faster and be more productive. **Color - Green**

3. **Identity** is the third and deepest inner layer. Students will list ideas on how to change any beliefs, biases, their self-image, and any judgment students have against themselves or others which may affect and determine their ability as a student. **Color - Red**

Brain Power (Page 52 in *The RGP: Student Edition*)

Habit activation in the brain takes place in the students' **Medial Prefrontal Cortex** which stores long-term assessments of their environmental experiences. In contrast, their short-term memories are actively embedded into their **Hippocampus**. Impulse control is located in the **Dorsolateral Prefrontal Cortex** and in the **Anterior Cingulate Cortex**.

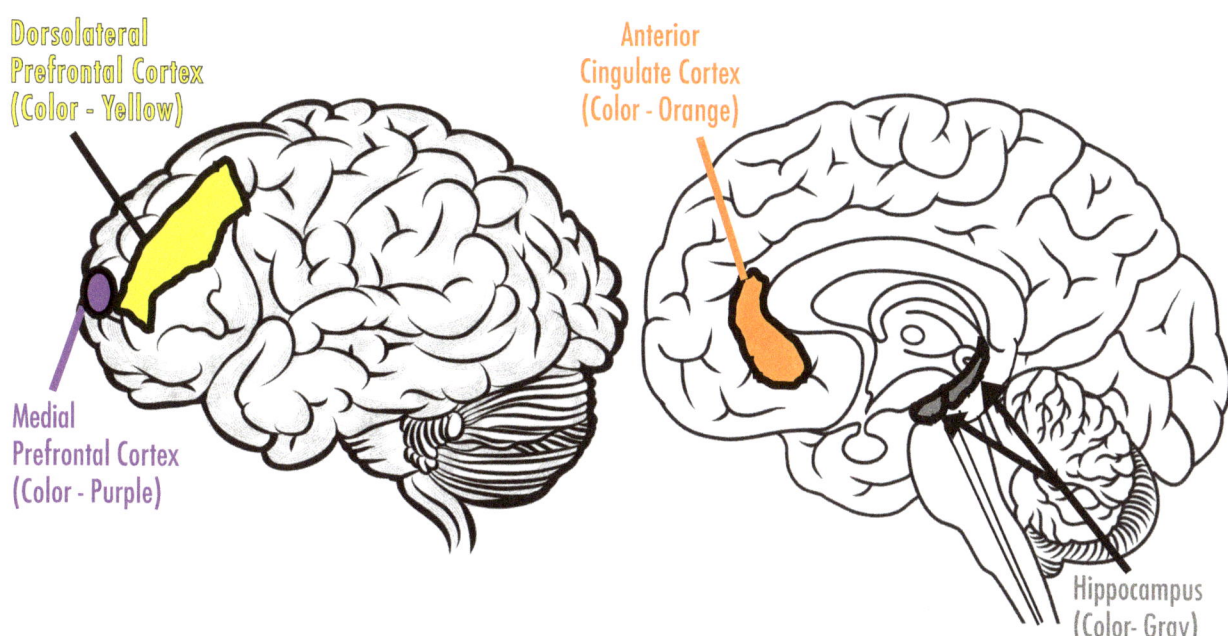

Dorsolateral Prefrontal Cortex (Color - Yellow)

Anterior Cingulate Cortex (Color - Orange)

Medial Prefrontal Cortex (Color - Purple)

Hippocampus (Color - Gray)

Cognitive Skills

• **Talking Points for Cognitive Skills Section:** (Page 53 in *The RGP: Student Edition*)

Step #2: Gauging Your Feelings

How You May Feel About Breaking a Habit:

10. Extreme anxiety/I feel extreme distress with change.
9. Very anxious/ I feel extremely overwhelmed with change.
8. High anxiety/My heart is racing thinking about change.
7. Moderate-to-high anxiety/I am afraid of a set back.
6. Moderately anxious/I've encountered a roadblock.
5. Mild-to-moderate anxiety/I'm making progress with a new habit.
4. Mild anxiety/I feel ready for something new.
3. Minimal anxiety/I will read about why new habits are good.
2. Feeling good/I feel like I can extend myself and grow.
1. I love learning new things.

Step #3: Overcoming Obstacles

Creating a New Habit to Wake Up Early:

10. I now wake up on my own before my alarm goes off.
9. I will leave for school early so I don't have to rush.
8. I will set the tone of my day with calming breathing exercises.
7. I will go outside to see the sun and set my circadian rhythm.
6. I will drink a glass of ice water to wake up my inner body.
5. I will wake up and splash cold water on my face.
4. I will set my alarm to go off at the same time every day.
3. I will watch funny online videos about morning routines.
2. I will watch a movie about a person that is a morning person.
1. I will listen to an upbeat song about starting your day early.

If any information in this playbook is upsetting, please talk to a parent/guardian, school counselor, teacher, or medical professional.
This book is sold with the understanding that the publisher and the author are not engaged in rendering medical, legal, or other professional advice or services.
If professional assistance is required, the services of a competent professional should be sought.

• What is Your Legacy? - Core Values •

> **FOR LESSON PLANNING PURPOSES - AMOUNT OF TIME TO ALLOCATE: 25 minutes**
> *Add 4 minutes to take the Reflections Publishing Communication Assessment/Add time to the Mindfulness section (if possible), as 20 minutes provides optimal benefits.
> - 4114U and Student Activity - 6 minutes PLUS Class Discussion - 8 minutes
> - Playbook Strategy #1: Understanding Brain Power - 1 minute
> - Playbook Strategy #2: Learning Cognitive Strategies - 10 minutes
>   - Step #1 Expressive Writing - 2 minutes
>   - Step #2: Gauging Your Feelings - 4 minutes
>   - Step #3 Overcoming Obstacles - 4 minutes
> - Playbook Strategy #3: Learning Communication Strategies - 1 minute
>   - *Reflections Publishing Communication Assessment - 4 minutes
> - Playbook Strategy #4: Learning Mindfulness Strategies - 2 minutes
> - Playbook Strategy #5: Developing New Habits - 2 minutes
> - Playbook Strategy #6: Anxiety-Buster To-Do List - 1 minute

• Facilitator Talking Points: (Page 56 in *The RGP: Student Edition*)

1. Encourage students to decide who they are, what they stand for, and their core values. Their values, morals, and beliefs will steer them in the direction in which they will live their life. While having trust-worthy mentors along the way will help guide and advise them—only they can decide who they want to be someday.

2. The prefrontal cortex part of the preteen/teenage brain continues to develop into their twenties—with some even saying the prefrontal cortex for males is not fully developed until 30-years-old. The prefrontal cortex is the part of the brain where deductive reasoning and decision-making skills develop. While this decision-making part of the brain continues to develop into a young adult's second decade of life, it is known that an individual learns the difference between right and wrong by the age of five-years-old.

3. **In addition to acquiring strong communication skills, a successful person needs to have a good attitude, a strong hard work ethic, be committed to showing up, being on time—always kind and respectful, and most importantly, you need to have common sense. You can be the smartest person in the world, but if you are lacking strong communication skills and do not have common sense, then you will struggle in life.**

4. Emphasize to students that while their goals may shift throughout their lives, the values and morals they learned are embedded into their personality and will guide them to create their value system. This system may fall into the following categories: Community Service, Family Values, Spiritual Values, and Work Ethic.

• Legacy/Core Values Student Activity: (Page 57 in *The RGP: Student Edition*)

Have students spend some time reflecting, helping them align their morals, priorities, and values. Encourage students to follow their gut reactions when they read the following questions and write those thoughts down. Provide Post-it notes to students to have them write their main thoughts and goals onto a Post-it to put in their locker or notebook or to make as a screensaver on their cell phone.

1. **What does having common sense mean to you?**
2. **What are you doing now that will create your future legacy?**
3. **If money were no obstacle, who and what would you be someday?**
4. **What steps can you take to make that dream happen?**

Brain Power (Page 58 in *The RGP: Student Edition*)

Researchers Falk & Scholz (2018) conducted a meta-analysis of neuroimaging studies that highlighted how the **Ventral Striatum (VS)** and parts of the **Ventromedial Prefrontal Cortex (VMPFC)** play a role in how a person calculates their core values. The **VS** and **VMPFC** analyze a person's decision-making process that ultimately contributes to their final decisions, preferences, and actions. Individuals who create their core values and personal legacy can choose how they prefer to communicate and if they will conform to their peers' influence.

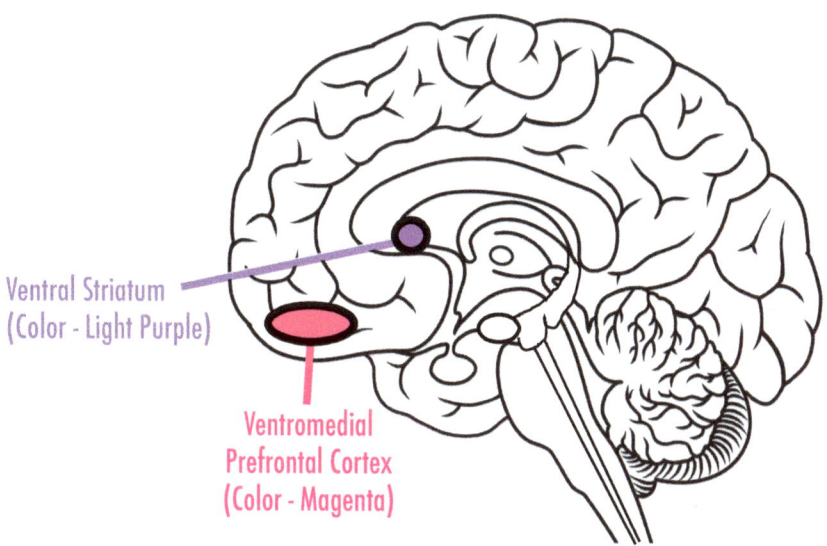

Ventral Striatum (Color - Light Purple)

Ventromedial Prefrontal Cortex (Color - Magenta)

Cognitive Skills

- **Talking Points for Cognitive Skills Section:** (Page 59 in *The RGP: Student Edition*)

Step #2: Gauging Your Feelings

How Do You Feel About Your Core Values?:

10. Extreme anxiety/I feel extreme distress with no values.
9. Very anxious/ I feel overwhelmed with no core values.
8. High anxiety/My heart is racing about what I stand for.
7. Moderate-to-high anxiety/I lie about my core values.
6. Moderately anxious/I can't stand up for my core values.
5. Mild-to-moderate anxiety/I don't like apologizing for my values.
4. Mild anxiety/I will read about core values and beliefs.
3. Minimal anxiety/I feel like I can broaden core values.
2. Feeling good/I feel confident in my core values.
1. No anxiety/I am extremely confident and know who I am.

Step #3: Overcoming Obstacles

Ideas for Fears of Forming My Core Values?:

10. I will be a mentor to others on how to stand up for beliefs.
9. I will join a group that shares my same core values.
8. I will join a group that supports and encourages me.
7. I will do breathing exercises to overcome judgment.
6. I will practice "I am" statements to strengthen beliefs.
5. I will find a friend who thinks like me.
4. I will learn tools to help me be resilient with core values.
3. I will watch funny online videos about making good choices.
2. I will watch a movie about a person deciding who they are.
1. I will listen to an upbeat song about who I am.

If any information in this playbook is upsetting, please talk to a parent/guardian, school counselor, teacher, or medical professional.

This book is sold with the understanding that the publisher and the author are not engaged in rendering medical, legal, or other professional advice or services. If professional assistance is required, the services of a competent professional should be sought.

• Who Are Your Mentors/Coaches? •

FOR LESSON PLANNING PURPOSES - AMOUNT OF TIME TO ALLOCATE: 25 minutes
*Add 4 minutes to take the Reflections Publishing Communication Assessment/Add time to the Mindfulness section (if possible), as 20 minutes provides optimal benefits.

- • 4114U and Student Activity - 6 minutes PLUS Class Discussion - 8 minutes
- Playbook Strategy #1: Understanding Brain Power - 1 minute
- Playbook Strategy #2: Learning Cognitive Strategies - 10 minutes
  - Step #1 Expressive Writing - 2 minutes
  - Step #2: Gauging Your Feelings - 4 minutes
  - Step #3 Overcoming Obstacles - 4 minutes
- Playbook Strategy #3: Learning Communication Strategies - 1 minute
  - *Reflections Publishing Communication Assessment - 4 minutes
- Playbook Strategy #4: Learning Mindfulness Strategies - 2 minutes
- Playbook Strategy #5: Developing New Habits - 2 minutes
- Playbook Strategy #6: Anxiety-Buster To-Do List - 1 minute

• Facilitator Talking Points: (Page 62 in *The RGP: Student Edition*)

- According to Jack et al. (2013), when individuals have mentors and coaches, the Positive Emotional Attractor (PEA) is activated in their brain. Neural brain circuits are activated, allowing students to think more positively and stay motivated. They can visually picture their success and the path they need to take to achieve their goals.

- Boyatzis (2008) indicates that when individuals receive effective coaching, the Intentional Change Theory comes into play—creating a behavioral change. Boyatzis & Akrivou (2006) believe when a teen's mentor and/or coach utilizes the Intentional Change Theory, they are encouraging students to find the following qualities in themselves:

  - • What is your ideal self?
  - • What is your calling and purpose, and what choices should you make to stay on this track?
  - • What are your core values, philosophy, and your personal self and identity?
  - • What are your passions in life?

- Conner & Pope (2013) believe the goal for every student is to connect with at least one teacher so you can receive any necessary resources to implement strategies to help reduce stress.

- Colarossi and Eccles (2003) also support the notion of teens finding mentors outside of their family circle, which will help them to form a secure sense of self.

- Phillippo et al. (2017) agree that while you may have a supportive family network, receiving advice and feedback from a mentor will help you form your self-concept and identity formation.

- Erickson et al. (2009) state that you will build resiliency when you have trustworthy and nurturing adults in your life, who are not in your immediate family circle.

• Mentoring Steps Student Activity: (Pages 62-63 in *The RGP: Student Edition*)

- Students can create a dot-to-dot of a mountain with the steps they need to take to achieve their goals and how a mentor can assist with addressing any necessary steps and/or setbacks they might experience along the way.
- Students are asked to trace or draw a picture of their hand on **page 63** and write the names of five individuals who they consider to be a coach, cheerleader, or mentor in their life. They are to only list people outside their immediate family (e.g., teacher, coach, aunt or uncle.).

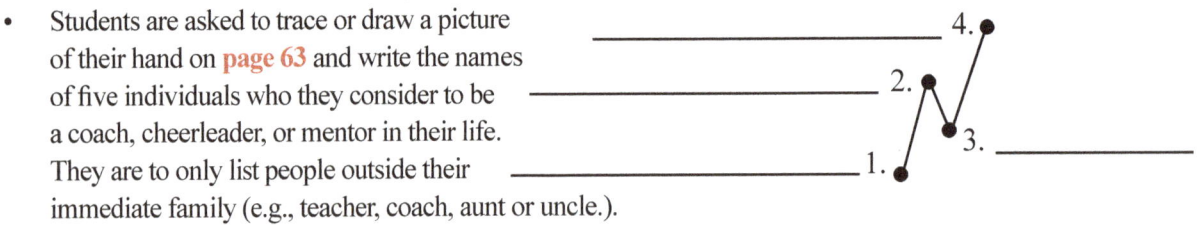

-64-

Brain Power (Page 64 in *The RGP: Student Edition*)

As noted in *The RGP: Student Edition* on page 62, in the research article by Jack et al. (2013), their findings indicate that when individuals have mentors and coaches, the Positive Emotional Attractor (PEA) is activated in the brain. Thus, the neural brain circuits activated are the Lateral Occipital Cortex, Superior Temporal Cortex, Medial Parietal, Subgenual Cingulate, Nucleus Accumbens, and left Lateral Prefrontal Cortex.

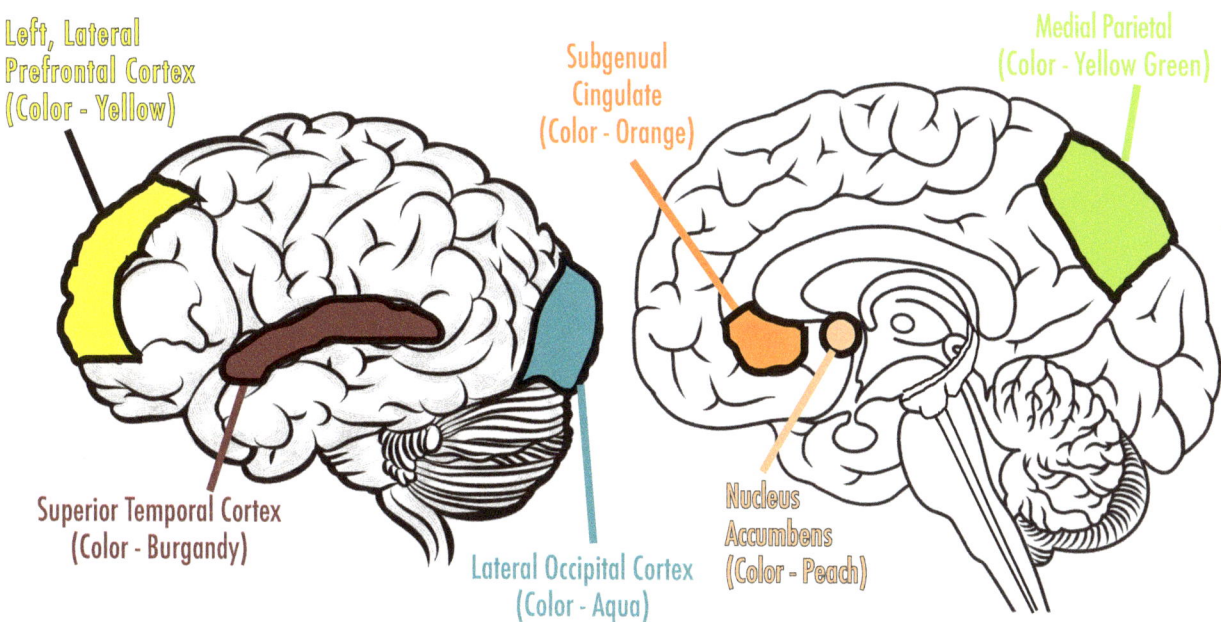

Cognitive Skills

- **Talking Points for Cognitive Skills Section:** (Page 65 in *The RGP: Student Edition*)

Step #2: Gauging Your Feelings

How Do Feel About Your Support System?:

10. Extreme anxiety/I have no mentors in my life.
9. Very anxious/ I'm not having success finding mentors.
8. High anxiety/I don't know who to ask to be a mentor.
7. Moderate-to-high anxiety/I'll ask a mentor based on goals.
6. Moderately anxious/I will try to network to find a mentor.
5. Mild-to-moderate anxiety/I will join clubs to find a mentor.
4. Mild anxiety/I will reach out to potential mentors.
3. Minimal anxiety/I'm working to make mentor connections.
2. Feeling good/I think I have five mentors in my life.
1. No anxiety/I have five people I consider mentors to me.

Step #3: Overcoming Obstacles

Ideas for Fear of Finding Support System:

10. They said, "Yes!" I'm extremely grateful to find five mentors.
9. Send thank you note after meeting your possible mentor.
8. Approach your possible mentor with confidence to ask them.
7. Prepare and practice for the conversation with possible mentor.
6. Request and schedule a meeting with potential mentor.
5. Create a script in how you will ask someone to be a mentor.
4. Prioritize the list of potential mentors to ask.
3. List a list of potential mentors to ask.
2. Research and reflect on potential mentors to ask.
1. Watch a movie about a coach or mentor in a teen's life.

If any information in this playbook is upsetting, please talk to a parent/guardian, school counselor, teacher, or medical professional.
This book is sold with the understanding that the publisher and the author are not engaged in rendering medical, legal, or other professional advice or services.
If professional assistance is required, the services of a competent professional should be sought.

Section Seven

What's Your Game Plan?

Life Choices

(Page 69 in *The RGP: Student Edition*)

LIFE TOPICS:

- Self and Identity - 70
- Social Media - Setting Boundaries - 76
- Time Management - Life Balance - 82

*Student Edition Pages

• Self and Identity •

> **FOR LESSON PLANNING PURPOSES - AMOUNT OF TIME TO ALLOCATE: 28 minutes**
> *Add 4 minutes to take the Reflections Publishing Communication Assessment/Add time to the Mindfulness section (if possible), as 20 minutes provides optimal benefits.
> - 4114U and Student Activity - 5 minutes PLUS Class Discussion - 7 minutes
> - Playbook Strategy #1: Understanding Brain Power - 1 minute
> - Playbook Strategy #2: Learning Cognitive Strategies - 10 minutes
>   - Step #1 Expressive Writing - 2 minutes
>   - Step #2: Gauging Your Feelings - 4 minutes
>   - Step #3 Overcoming Obstacles - 4 minutes
> - Playbook Strategy #3: Learning Communication Strategies - 2 minutes
>   - *Reflections Publishing Communication Assessment - 4 minutes
> - Playbook Strategy #4: Learning Mindfulness Strategies - 5 minutes
> - Playbook Strategy #5: Developing New Habits - 2 minutes
> - Playbook Strategy #6: Anxiety-Buster To-Do List - 1 minute

• Facilitator Talking Points: (Page 70 in *The RGP: Student Edition*)

This topic of Self and Identity follows the concept of "What is Your Legacy? - Core Values" nicely. Arkes & Kajdasz (2011) states: **"A stable essence or core that predicts their behavior, that who they are matter for what they do, and that what they do reflects who they are."**

Arnett (2018) defines identity as a period of time in an adolescent's life when they tend to self-assess **who they are** (their abilities and characteristics), **what they believe** (their belief system and core values), **how they get along** with others (their personal relations), and **where/how do they fit** (into the world around them).

When students try to define themselves, they typically want to describe themselves with stable and consistent traits in mind. Individuals usually use adjectives and action verbs to describe themselves (English & Chen). Utilizing a Self-Evaluation Maintenance (SEM) Model of Social Behavior formulation by Tesser (1988), a positive sense of self-esteem can emerge when "both stability and changeability" are part of the equation. **This SEM Model is comprised of two dynamic processes:**
- **The reflection process**
- **The comparison process**

These two processes interact during self-evaluation in opposite ways, but both have the interactive quality of their predictions. According to Michael A. Hogg, part of a teenager's self and identity is associated with the social group at school they associate with because their peer group strongly influences:
- **How a teenager views themself and who they are as a person**
- **Their attitude and values**
- **Actions they take and how they assimilate into the world around them**

Throughout a learner's life, they will grow and evolve as they mature. As their educator and mentor, just remind them to always think for themself and not let their social identity with a group affect their behavior, decisions, and forming any unwanted biases and discrimination against others.

• Self and Identity Student Activity: (Page 71 in *The RGP: Student Edition*)

Thinking with a growth mindset, read the questions below and ask students how they see themselves today and how they would like to change going forward.

1. **Compassion Towards Yourself and Others:**
2. **Hobbies (i.e., Athleticism, Musically-Talented):**
3. **Intelligence:**
4. **Personality:**
5. **Make Your Own Category** _____

Brain Power (Page 72 in *The RGP: Student Edition*)

In a research report by McAdams & Krawczyk (2014) studying the different components of identity, different neuroimaging tasks showed participants conducting tasks related to social activities and physical appearance—through descriptive phrases. Both tasks consisted of reading and responding to statements with three different perspectives: Self, Friend, and Reflection. Significant differences were found in fMRI activation channels relating to self-knowledge ('I am', 'I look') and perspective-taking ('I believe', 'Friend believes') statements in the Precuneus, along with two areas of the Dorsal Anterior Cingulate, and the left Medial (middle) Frontal Gyrus.

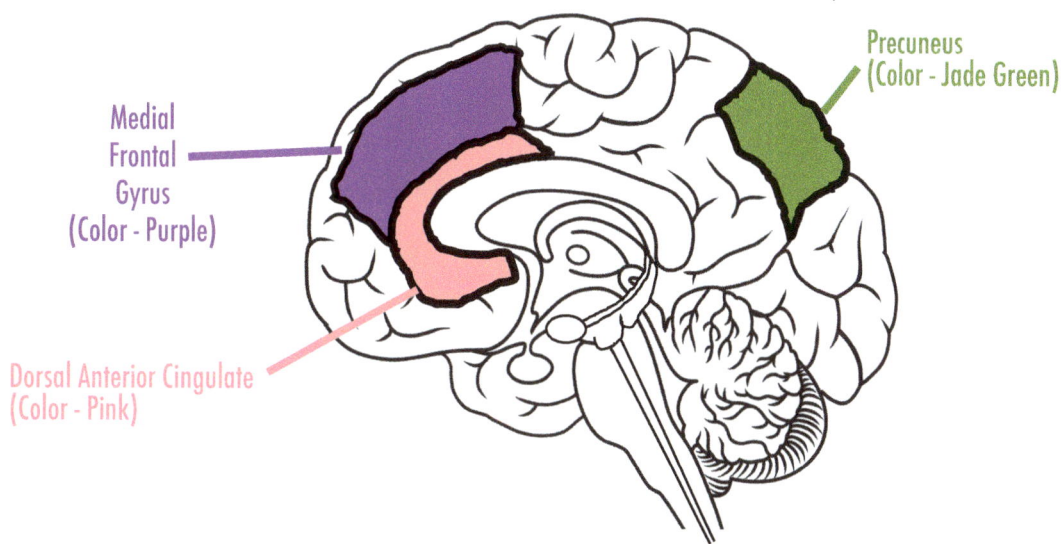

Cognitive Skills

• **Talking Points for Cognitive Skills Section:** (Page 73 in *The RGP: Student Edition*)

Step #2: Gauging Your Feelings

How Do Feel About Your Sense of Self?

10. Extreme anxiety/I'm having a panic attack; Who am I?
9. Very anxious/My heart is racing; I'm having an identity crisis.
8. High anxiety/I feel like have a good sense of self.
7. Moderate-to-high anxiety/ What is my identity?
6. Moderately anxious/I don't know my next steps.
5. Mild-to-moderate anxiety/I feel I'm comparing myself.
4. Mild anxiety/I think traveling might expand my sense of self.
3. Minimal anxiety/I know who I am; my life is on track.
2. Feeling good/I feel I am secure with my sense of self.
1. No anxiety/I feel confident and know who I am.

Step #3: Overcoming Obstacles

Thoughts on Identifying Your Sense of Self

10. I will teach a class on Self and Identity.
9. I will take a class and gain a better sense of myself.
8. I will discuss with a friend about personal self and identity.
7. I will read books about on the topic Self and Identity.
6. I will practice "I am" statements to increase my confidence.
5. I will meet with a counselor to help with my self and identity.
4. I will journal about movies I've watched on self and identity.
3. I will watch online funny videos about identity crisis.
2. I will watch a movie about soul searching.
1. I will listen to an upbeat song about self-contentment.

If any information in this playbook is upsetting, please talk to a parent/guardian, school counselor, teacher, or medical professional.
This book is sold with the understanding that the publisher and the author are not engaged in rendering medical, legal, or other professional advice or services.
If professional assistance is required, the services of a competent professional should be sought.

•Social Media - Setting Boundaries•

> **FOR LESSON PLANNING PURPOSES - AMOUNT OF TIME TO ALLOCATE: 35 minutes**
> *Add 4 minutes to take the Reflections Publishing Communication Assessment/Add time to the Mindfulness section (if possible), as 20 minutes provides optimal benefits.
> - 4114U and Student Activity - 6 minutes PLUS Class Discussion - 10 minutes
> - Playbook Strategy #1: Understanding Brain Power - 1 minute
> - Playbook Strategy #2: Learning Cognitive Strategies - 10 minutes
>   - Step #1 Expressive Writing - 2 minutes
>   - Step #2 Gauging Your Feelings - 4 minutes
>   - Step #3 Overcoming Obstacles - 4 minutes
> - Playbook Strategy #3: Learning Communication Strategies - 6 minutes
>   - *Reflections Publishing Communication Assessment - 4 minutes
> - Playbook Strategy #4: Learning Mindfulness Strategies - 5 minutes
> - Playbook Strategy #5: Developing New Habits - 2 minutes
> - Playbook Strategy #6: Anxiety-Buster To-Do List - 1 minute

- **Facilitator Talking Points:** (Page 76 in *The RGP: Student Edition*)
    - The Child Mind Institute states teenagers and young adults are the individuals who are the most avid and intense users of social media. The concern for this age group is that their brain is forming, and social media can negatively affect their self-esteem and trigger self-harm ideation.
    - The Child Mind Institute believes too much screen time is also associated with insufficient sleep, with anxiety also linked to the onset of mental health symptoms.
    - The Child Mind Institute indicates that teenagers and young adults constantly using social media increase their chances of developing depression from between 13 to 66 percent.
    - Twenge et al. (2018) state that since 2010, screen time and mental health issues have continued trending upward—with adolescent depression and self-harm highly linked; 33 percent increase in depressive symptoms in eighth-through twelfth-grade students and the female suicide rate also increased.
    - Social media and cell phone time can be a massive source of distraction and procrastination—distracting students from their homework and harming their academic performance.
    - Social media can portray a distorted reality, making students feel unnecessarily insecure.
    - People can use apps to make their pictures perfect. Most of what you see on social media is not real.
    - Social media opens the door to students feeling inferior, jealous, and envious of others when, in fact, they might be comparing themselves to a fake picture or photoshopped image.
    - Social media can also interfere with a student's sleep schedule as the blue light emitted from their computer and cell phone disrupts melatonin production—the hormone that helps them fall asleep.
    - Not getting enough sleep on a nightly basis causes fatigue—leading to poor concentration at school.

    Here are some ways that students can use social media in a healthy manner:
    1. Set a timer to limit the amount of time you spend on social media.
    2. Make sure to follow accounts that only leave you feeling good about yourself.
    3. Write positive things when commenting on a person's post—writing what you would say face-to-face.

- **Social Media Student Activity:** (Page 77 in *The RGP: Student Edition*)

    Social media can be a powerful tool—keeping us connected and sharing valuable ideas. However, what you see on social media may be an edited version of reality. Students should answer the following questions:
    1. **List ways that social media is helpful:**
    2. **List some ways that social media is harmful to their self-esteem:**
    3. **What to keep in mind when scrolling through social media accounts:**
    4. **Doodle and Draw:**

- **Communications Activity on Social Media:** (Page 80 in *The RGP: Student Edition*)

    As a class or working in groups, help students practice complimenting each other and spreading kindness.

Brain Power (Page 74 in *The RGP: Student Edition*)

A research study analyzing social feedback processing in adolescents highlighted increased brain activity in the Dorsal Medial Prefrontal Cortex, Anterior Cingulate Cortex, and Bilateral Insula areas. The report emphasized that neuroimaging captured how females in their late adolescent years change their behavior based on feedback from their peers. The findings indicated a significant association between media-by-peer interactions and a female's future interpretation of an ideal female body.

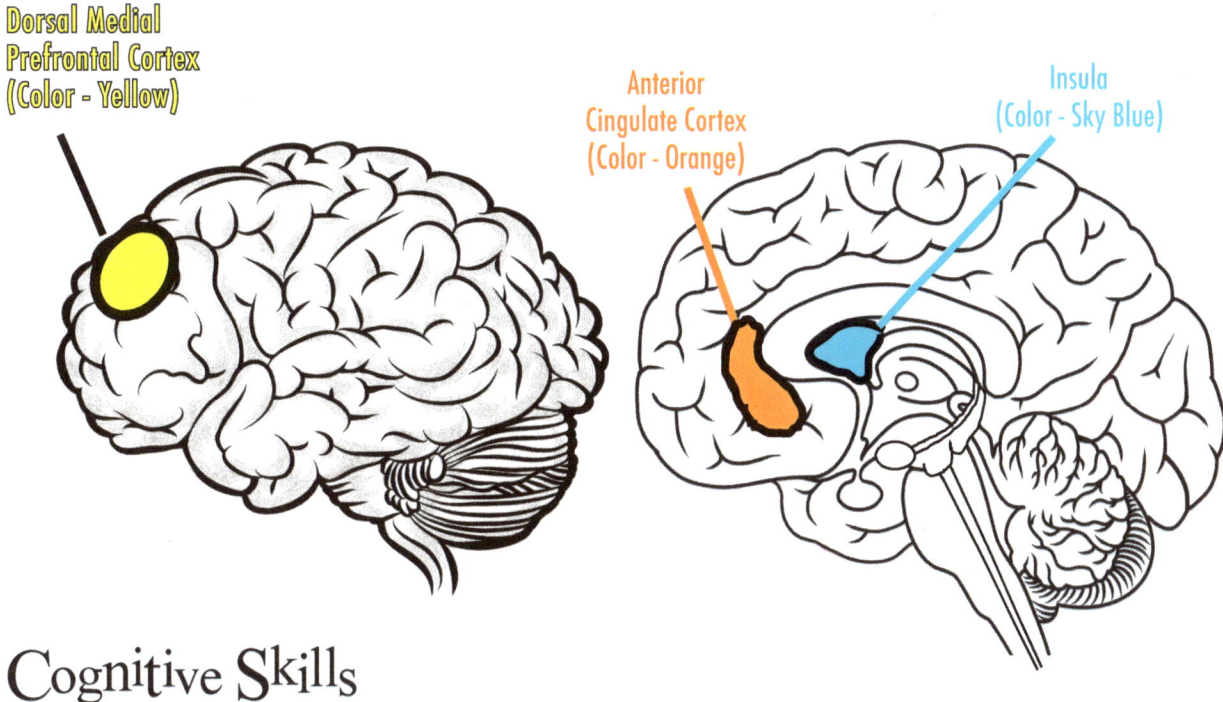

Dorsal Medial Prefrontal Cortex (Color - Yellow)

Anterior Cingulate Cortex (Color - Orange)

Insula (Color - Sky Blue)

Cognitive Skills

• **Talking Points for Cognitive Skills Section:** (Page 79 in *The RGP: Student Edition*)

Step #2: Gauging Your Feelings

How you May Feel About Social Media

10. Extreme anxiety/I'm having a panic attack about no "likes."
9. Very anxious/My heart is racing. I'm afraid of FOMO.
8. High anxiety/I feel like everyone is judging me online.
7. Moderate-to-high anxiety/I feel overwhelmed and uneasy.
6. Moderately anxious/I feel very self-conscious with my posts.
5. Mild-to-moderate anxiety/I feel okay about social media.
4. Mild anxiety/I think social media is a waste of time.
3. Minimal anxiety/I feel I have good social media boundaries.
2. Feeling good/I feel I have a good balance in life.
1. No anxiety/I feel confident in my social media presence.

Step #3: Overcoming Obstacles

Ideas on Overcoming Social Media Fears

10. I am confident in sharing pictures on social media.
9. I longer worry about people judging me.
8. I will not compare myself to others on social media.
7. I will stay away from possible online scams.
6. I will educate myself on cyberbullying.
5. I will stay away from posts that make me feel bad.
4. I will follow positive social media platforms.
3. I will watch online videos about social fears as a teenager.
2. I will watch a movie about middle/high school social fears.
1. I will listen to an upbeat song about overcoming fears.

If any information in this playbook is upsetting, please talk to a parent/guardian, school counselor, teacher, or medical professional.
This book is sold with the understanding that the publisher and the author are not engaged in rendering medical, legal, or other professional advice or services.
If professional assistance is required, the services of a competent professional should be sought.

• Time Management - Life Balance •

> **FOR LESSON PLANNING PURPOSES - AMOUNT OF TIME TO ALLOCATE: 23 minutes**
> *Add 4 minutes to take the Reflections Publishing Communication Assessment/Add time to the Mindfulness section (if possible), as 20 minutes provides optimal benefits.
>
> - 4114U and Student Activity - 3 minutes PLUS Class Discussion - 5 minutes
> - Playbook Strategy #1: Understanding Brain Power - 1 minute
> - Playbook Strategy #2: Learning Cognitive Strategies - 10 minutes
>   - Step #1 Expressive Writing - 2 minutes
>   - Step #2: Gauging Your Feelings - 4 minutes
>   - Step #3 Overcoming Obstacles - 4 minutes
> - Playbook Strategy #3: Learning Communication Strategies - 1 minute
>   - *Reflections Publishing Communication Assessment - 4 minutes
> - Playbook Strategy #4: Learning Mindfulness Strategies - 3 minutes
> - Playbook Strategy #5: Developing New Habits - 2 minutes
> - Playbook Strategy #6: Anxiety-Buster To-Do List - 1 minute

• Facilitator Talking Points: (Page 82 in *The RGP: Student Edition*)

- Life is all about balance and choices regarding how to should spend your time. When you create a schedule and get your work done either early or on time, you will be less stressed.
- Learning and gaining strong time management skills takes a lot of time and practice.
- Remind students to be kind and patient with themselves and stay committed to reaching their goals.
- Help students celebrate their successes and accomplishments as they progress through this list.

Here are Some Time Management Tips for Students to Try:

1. As listed as Playbook Strategy #6: Anxiety Buster To-Do List, **when students break down their tasks into smaller steps, it can help relieve anxiety.** Once they put a task on their To-Do List, it frees their brain to spend energy toward that task and be more creative.

2. **Minimize distractions** and find a place where students can focus clearly.

3. For students to stay on track with their goals, they need to learn what they have time to do now and what they need to save for later. There are only so many hours in the day, so they must learn to say "no" to some things. Our bodies break down and get sick if we try to be Superman or Superwoman. Students should remember **they are only human, so they should keep realistic expectations of themselves.**

4. **Avoid multi-tasking;** focus on one thing at a time and do it well. When students try to do too many things at once, they chase their tails in a circle like a dog.

. . . .

• Time Management Student Activity: (Page 83 in *The RGP: Student Edition*)

- **List Your Game Plan to Achieve a Strong Life Balance and Time Management Skills:**

- **Doodle or Draw to Help Process Balancing Your Time:**

Brain Power (Page 84 in *The RGP: Student Edition*)

The **Posterior Cingulate Cortex (PCC)** mediates the students' internally-generated thought processes they experience during emotional and social events. The **PCC** also includes self-directed cognitions and future planning, which is helpful with time management skills.

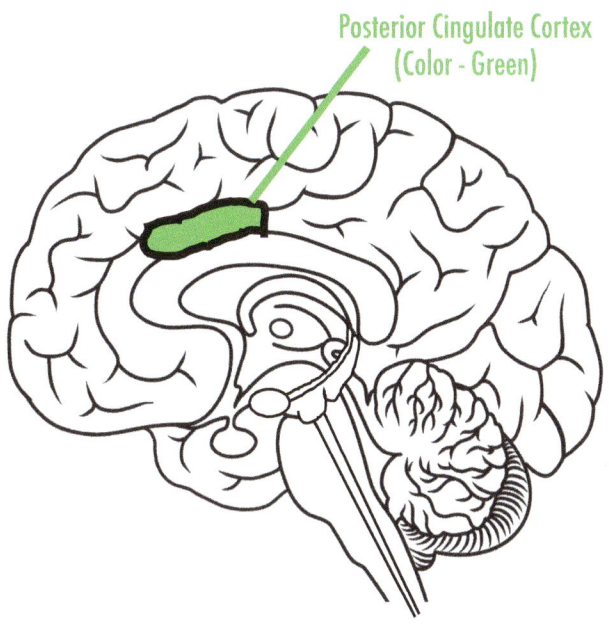

Posterior Cingulate Cortex (Color - Green)

Cognitive Skills

• **Talking Points for Cognitive Skills Section:** (Page 85 in *The RGP: Student Edition*)

Step #2: Gauging Your Feelings

How you May Feel About Time Management

10. Extreme anxiety/There are not enough hours in the day.
9. Very anxious/I'm having a panic attack—too much to do.
8. High anxiety/I study all the time and I'm still not prepared.
7. Moderate-to-high anxiety/I feel overwhelmed with school.
6. Moderately anxious/I don't feel like I studied enough.
5. Mild-to-moderate anxiety/I feel out of control.
4. Mild anxiety/I think I need to reorganize my day.
3. Minimal anxiety/I feel like my life is in a groove.
2. Feeling good/I feel organized and ready for the day.
1. No anxiety/I feel confident in my time management skills.

Step #3: Overcoming Obstacles

Overcoming Fears of No Life Balance

10. I'm confident with achieving my goals in a set amount of time.
9. I will write out my goals to get tasks done on time.
8. I will go outside and journal on ways to balance my life.
7. I will do the breathing exercise to help me focus.
6. I will practice "I am" statements to help balance my life.
5. I will work with a counselor to help with making a schedule.
4. I will join a study group to stay on track with my studies.
3. I will watch online videos about how to balance life.
2. I will watch a movie about balancing everything in life.
1. I will listen to an upbeat song about being overwhelmed.

If any information in this playbook is upsetting, please talk to a parent/guardian, school counselor, teacher, or medical professional.
This book is sold with the understanding that the publisher and the author are not engaged in rendering medical, legal, or other professional advice or services.
If professional assistance is required, the services of a competent professional should be sought.

Section Eight

What's Your Game Plan?

Life Crises

(Page 89 in *The RGP: Student Edition*)

LIFE TOPICS:

- Abuse - Domestic, Physical, and Verbal - 90
- Anxiety - 96
- Depression - 102
- Self-Harm - 108
- Substance Abuse - Alcohol and Drugs - 114

*Student Edition Pages

• Abuse - Domestic, Physical, and Verbal •

FOR LESSON PLANNING PURPOSES - AMOUNT OF TIME TO ALLOCATE: 30 minutes
*Add 4 minutes to take the Reflections Publishing Communication Assessment/Add time to the Mindfulness section (if possible), as 20 minutes provides optimal benefits.

- 4114U and Student Activity - 6 minutes PLUS Class Discussion - 10 minutes
- Playbook Strategy #1: Understanding Brain Power - 2 minutes
- Playbook Strategy #2: Learning Cognitive Strategies - 10 minutes
  - Step #1 Expressive Writing - 2 minutes
  - Step #2: Gauging Your Feelings - 4 minutes
  - Step #3 Overcoming Obstacles - 4 minutes
- Playbook Strategy #3: Learning Communication Strategies - 3 minutes
  - *Reflections Publishing Communication Assessment - 4 minutes
- Playbook Strategy #4: Learning Mindfulness Strategies - 2 minutes
- Playbook Strategy #5: Developing New Habits - 2 minutes
- Playbook Strategy #6: Anxiety-Buster To-Do List - 1 minute

• Facilitator Talking Points: (Page 90 in *The RGP: Student Edition*)

Emphasize to students **it is never okay for someone to abuse them**. Whether it is maltreatment, neglect, peer abuse, physical abuse, psychological/mental abuse, or sexual abuse—**not even one time is okay.** If they do not leave the first time someone abuses them, they may never leave. Nontouching ("peeping Tom") and nonverbal (seething glare) are also abuse. The "Communication Skills" section will provide students with talking points to seek help from a trusted adult.

In 2019, in a Child Maltreatment Report released by the U.S. Department of Health & Human Services, Administration for Children and Families divided almost eight million reported cases of child abuse into the following four categories: neglect (74.9%), Physical abuse (17.5%), Sexual abuse (9.3%), and Psychological maltreatment (6.1%). According to Zielinski (2009), in a United States childhood maltreatment study with a large sample size of 5,004 participants, this researcher reported that 34.6% of participants experienced child maltreatment.

A research study by Feiring, Taska, & Lewis (1999) shows that through different child development stages, victims will process their abuse experience both mentally and socially, and their brain will process the experience differently depending on the developmental period.

Sensitivity Periods and Risk Factors for Childhood Maltreatment

According to Heim et al. (2013), students must take abuse seriously because when children are exposed to early childhood adversity, they can experience significant neuroplastic changes in the cortex—based on the event's nature and sensitive developmental timing. The good thing is their brain will attempt to protect itself if they experience an aversive inappropriate event and will not allocate resources to registering the traumatic event. The brain will create adaptive responses to shield them from the abuse or adversity they are experiencing.

We cannot pretend abuse does not occur because, according to a community study conducted by Stein et al. (1997), they discovered that 74.2% of females and 81% of males reported exposure to one or more traumatic events in their lifetime.

Early detection for any at-risk child needs to be taken seriously because, for example, if parental verbal abuse starts at age three, an fMRI brain scan will likely show elevated gray matter in the left Superior Gyrus area (Auditory Cortex) based on studies by Choi et al. (2009) and a study by Tomoda et al. (2011) also showed reduced right Hippocampal volume in the abused brain. **The bottom line is that the "act of abuse" a person experiences will negatively affect the brain.**

• Abusive Situation Student Activity: (Page 91 in *The RGP: Student Edition*)

Have students draw and/or write out the steps they would take if they experienced abuse.

Brain Power (Page 92 in *The RGP: Student Edition*)

Students are instructed to go to **page 21 in** *The RGP: Student Edition* to color and label the following **bolded Cortex regions of the brain that are negatively affected by abuse:**

- See/Witness abuse → **Visual Cortex**
- Hear abuse → **Auditory Cortex**
- Smells during abuse → **Olfactory Cortex**
- Abusive Touch → **Somatosensory Cortex**

Lawson et al. (2017) state that childhood maltreatment can show a reduction in **Hippocampal** volume. Another research study by Heim et al. (2013) reports these changes include cortical thinning in a very specific brain region—mediating the brain's sensory perception and processing areas that are directly correlated to the specific abusive experiences.

Sexual abuse cases reported by Anderson et al. (2008) indicate the **Bilateral Hippocampal** volume showing significant negative alterations when children were exposed to sexual abuse at age 3- to 5-years-old and to a smaller degree in ages 11- to 13-years-old. In fMRI findings in sexual abuse cases by Heim et al. (2013), the **Somatosensory Cortex** layer shows thinning; this is due to the nature of the abuse and alterations in the **Visual Cortex** part of the brain region due to facial recognition by the child's abuser.

Per Heim et al. (2013), Witnessing domestic abuse, will show a reduction in gray matter volume in the **Visual Cortex**, as well as in the neural pathways connecting the visual and limbic systems.

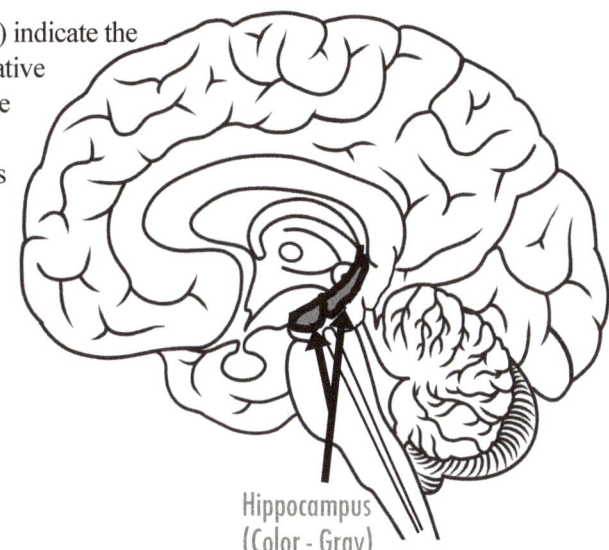

Hippocampus (Color - Gray)

Cognitive Skills

- **Talking Points for Cognitive Skills Section:** (Page 93 in *The RGP: Student Edition*)

Step #2: Gauging Your Feelings

How you May Feel About Verbal Abuse:

10. Extreme anxiety/I will burst if someone yells at me.
9. Very anxious/I'll have a panic attack if someone yells.
8. High anxiety/My heart begins racing if someone yells at me.
7. Moderate-to-high anxiety/I'm overwhelmed with yelling.
6. Moderately anxious/I am fearful of someone yelling.
5. Mild-to-moderate anxiety/I feel like someone is going to yell.
4. Mild anxiety/I know what to say if someone yells at me.
3. Minimal anxiety/I feel confident in standing up for myself.
2. Feeling good/I feel good in my relationships.
1. No anxiety/I feel confident in my relationships.

Step #3: Overcoming Obstacles

Ideas on Overcoming Verbal Abuse:

10. I am confident to stand up for myself against anyone.
9. I will do role-playing to practice standing up for myself.
8. I will journal ideas on what to say if someone yells at me.
7. I will do breathing exercise to help me to relax.
6. I will practice "I am" statements to increase my confidence.
5. I will work with a counselor to help give me tips and tools.
4. I will join a study group and identify what I still need to learn.
3. I will watch online videos about how to stand up for yourself.
2. I will watch a feel good movie about a functional family.
1. I will listen to an upbeat song about healthy relationships.

If you are experiencing an emergency, please seek immediate assistance from a parent/guardian, school counselor, teacher, or medical professional or call 911.

This book is sold with the understanding that the publisher and the author are not engaged in rendering medical, legal, or other professional advice or services. If professional assistance is required, the services of a competent professional should be sought.

• Anxiety •

> **FOR CLASS PLANNING PURPOSES - AMOUNT OF TIME TO ALLOCATE: 30 minutes**
> *Add 4 minutes to take the Reflections Publishing Communication Assessment/Add time to the Mindfulness section (if possible), as 20 minutes provides optimal benefits.
>
> - 4114U and Student Activity - 6 minutes PLUS Class Discussion - 9 minutes
> - Playbook Strategy #1: Understanding Brain Power - 1 minute
> - Playbook Strategy #2: Learning Cognitive Strategies - 10 minutes
>   - Step #1 Expressive Writing - 2 minutes
>   - Step #2: Gauging Your Feelings - 4 minutes
>   - Step #3 Overcoming Obstacles - 4 minutes
> - Playbook Strategy #3: Learning Communication Strategies - 3 minutes
>   - *Reflections Publishing Communication Assessment - 4 minutes
> - Playbook Strategy #4: Learning Mindfulness Strategies - 3 minutes
> - Playbook Strategy #5: Developing New Habits - 2 minutes
> - Playbook Strategy #6: Anxiety-Buster To-Do List - 1 minute

• Facilitator Talking Points: (Page 96 in *The RGP: Student Edition*)

- The good thing about anxiety is that it revs your body up like a car and is beneficial if you are in a dangerous situation because it initiates a fight-or-flight response in your body. This stress response releases cortisol in your brain—allowing your body to jump-start quickly and escape the threatening situation.

- The bad thing about anxiety is that your body cannot survive in a constant state of stress. This is not to say that a person's life is going to be perfect and easy every day, but adolescents also cannot stay stressed out either.

- Puberty is normally the time when anxiety is triggered in adolescents. According to a book by Jensen & Nutt (2015) called *The Teenage Brain*, due to the surge of puberty hormones, teenagers have a much more heightened response to stress than adults.

- This is why when students get stressed out about midterms or finals, they likely will get a headache, have an upset stomach, or catch a cold or the flu.

- Since the adolescent brain is actively growing, forming, and wiring itself, literally every day, their brain can either wire itself correctly and effectively or when episodes of extreme stress hit or substance abuse occurs (i.e., drugs and alcohol), the wiring can go awry—fraying and not connecting properly.

• Anxiety Student Activity: (Pages 96-97 in *The RGP: Student Edition*)

1. Students should turn to **page 114 in *The RGP: Student Edition*** and write the Two Rules listed at the top of the Substance Abuse: Drugs and Alcohol page.

2. Have a class discussion about how researchers who study test anxiety among adolescents found that mandala coloring was linked to an increased state of mindfulness and decreased test anxiety (Carsley & Heath, 2019; Rose & Lomas, 2020) on **page 96 in *The RGP: Student Edition***.

3. On **page 97 in *The RGP: Student Edition***, have students:
   Doodle, Draw Their Own Mandala, or Create a Dot•to•Dot:

Brain Power (Page 98 in *The RGP: Student Edition*)

Anxiety is a state where the sympathetic nervous system is stuck. In a research article about adolescents suffering from anxiety, the **Anterior Cingulate Cortex** region of the brain had hypo-activation in anxious adolescents and adults. "The unique U-shaped activation pattern in the **Ventromedial Prefrontal Cortex** in many anxious adolescents may reflect heightened sensitivity to threat and safety conditions."

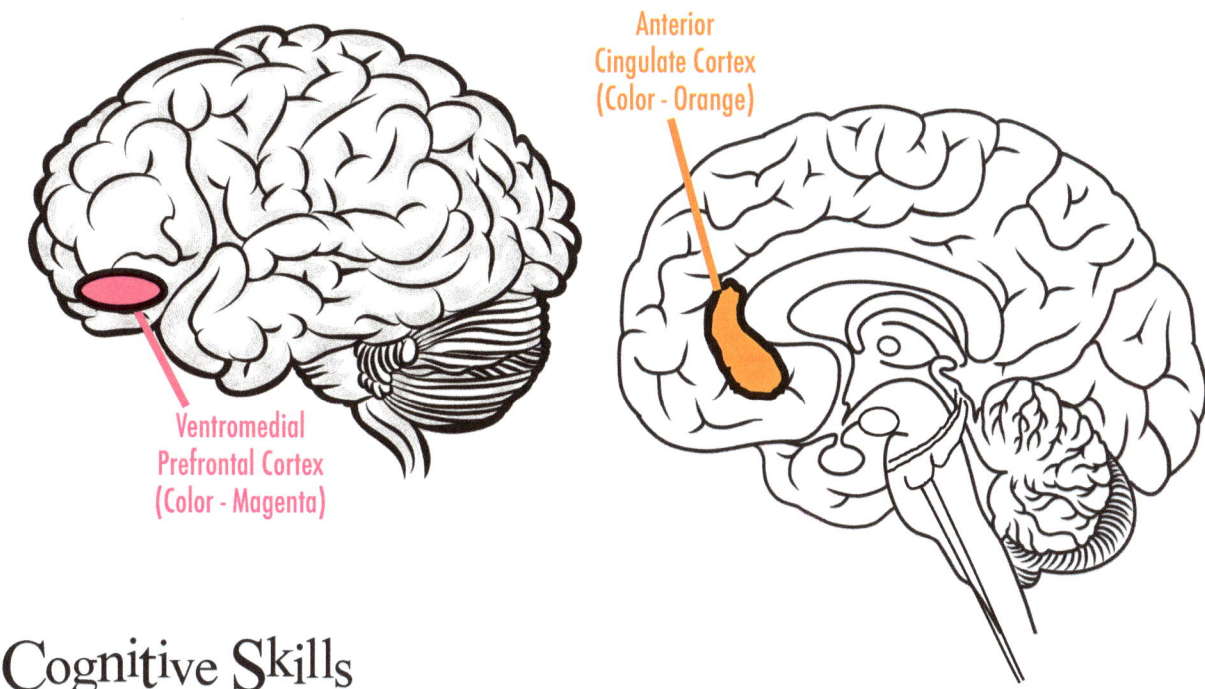

Anterior Cingulate Cortex (Color - Orange)

Ventromedial Prefrontal Cortex (Color - Magenta)

Cognitive Skills

- **Talking Points for Cognitive Skills Section:** (Page 99 in *The RGP: Student Edition*)

Step #2: Gauging Your Feelings

How you May Feel About Social Anxiety:

10. Extreme anxiety; panic or terror of a social situation
9. Very anxious; completely overwhelmed in a social situation
8. High anxiety; extremely tense in a social situation
7. Moderate-to-high anxiety; anxious in a social situation
6. Moderately anxious; intensely nervous in a social situation
5. Mild-to-moderate anxiety; extremely dreading a party
4. Mild anxiety; mildly nervous in a social situation
3. Minimal anxiety; slightly uncomfortable socially
2. Feeling good; looking forward to a social situation
1. No anxiety; completely relaxed in a social situation

Step #3: Overcoming Obstacles

Ideas to Overcome Social Anxiety Fears:

10. I am now confident attending party with no anxiety.
9. I will drive to the party with trusted friends.
8. I will role-play and practice things to say at the party.
7. I will journal ideas on things to say and do at the party.
6. I will go to a counselor to help deal with my social anxiety.
5. I will talk to a trusted friend about my social anxiety.
4. I will take a class on overcoming social anxiety.
3. I will watch online videos on overcoming social anxiety.
2. I will watch a movie about college parties.
1. I will listen to an upbeat song about going to a party.

If you are experiencing an emergency, please seek immediate assistance from a parent/guardian, school counselor, teacher, or medical professional or call 911.

This book is sold with the understanding that the publisher and the author are not engaged in rendering medical, legal, or other professional advice or services. If professional assistance is required, the services of a competent professional should be sought.

• Depression •

> **FOR LESSON PLANNING PURPOSES - AMOUNT OF TIME TO ALLOCATE: 30 minutes**
> *Add 4 minutes to take the Reflections Publishing Communication Assessment/Add time to the Mindfulness section (if possible), as 20 minutes provides optimal benefits.
>
> - 4114U and Student Activity - 7 minutes PLUS Class Discussion - 10 minutess
> - Playbook Strategy #1: Understanding Brain Power - 1 minute
> - Playbook Strategy #2: Learning Cognitive Strategies - 10 minutes
>   - Step #1 Expressive Writing - 2 minutes
>   - Step #2: Gauging Your Feelings - 4 minutes
>   - Step #3 Overcoming Obstacles - 4 minutes
> - Playbook Strategy #3: Learning Communication Strategies - 2 minutes
>   - *Reflections Publishing Communication Assessment - 4 minutes
> - Playbook Strategy #4: Learning Mindfulness Strategies - 4 minutes
> - Playbook Strategy #5: Developing New Habits - 2 minutes
> - Playbook Strategy #6: Anxiety-Buster To-Do List - 1 minute

• Facilitator Talking Points: (Page 102 in *The RGP: Student Edition*)

- Many times, anxiety and depression are co-morbid (i.e., two or more) symptoms.
- Puberty is the time when students might notice feeling anxious and/or depressed for the first time.
- Many body changes occur during puberty.
- Depression is a state of mind that affects many people at some point. For instance, when a loved one passes away, it is natural to feel depressed for approximately one year after this happens. If depression continues over one year, the student needs to address overcoming their depressive symptoms.
- The teenage brain is "plastic" and "livewired." The sooner students learn tips and tools to navigate their depression, the better their chance of a full recovery.
- The brain and body will always try to heal; students should not feel stuck in their emotional state.

• Brain Power Student Activity: (Page 104 in *The RGP: Student Edition*)

Students are instructed to use a **highlighter to mark the intervention results and areas of the brain affected** in each study below. They can refer back to **page 21 in *The RGP: Student Edition*** for the Human Brain Anatomy.

Approximately 33 percent of diagnosed adults with major depressive disorder know their depression started during their adolescent years (Goodyer et al., 2011). Hence, the importance of identifying at-risk adolescents during the ages of 11- to 17-years-old when brain maturation is at a significant developmental stage (Chattopadhyay et al., 2017). This has shown to be true in several research studies, including this study of 11- to 17-year-olds by Chattopadhyay et al. (2017) with 116 cross-sectional participants. At-risk designations were able to create potential intervention treatments. **Once intervention treatments were initiated, excellent results emerged—depression symptoms decreased and were represented in fMRI imaging in the brain's resting state Functional Communication (rsFC) networks.**

In a resting state fMRI study by Straub et al. (2017), 38 participants, ages 13- to 18-years-old, with healthy controls and adolescents with depression, received brain scans before receiving group Cognitive Skills Training sessions. **Teenagers with depression illustrated an enhanced Amygdala and a sgACC connectivity** with regions of the DMN. When depressed adolescents are compared before (pre-Cognitive Skills Training) to after (post-Cognitive Skills Training), the **brain scans show that functional connectivity significantly increased between the Amygdala and the left Dorsolateral PFC, Bilateral Dorsal ACC, and the left Anterior Insula**. This proves doing the **Cognitive Skills Training in *The Resilience Game Plan* will significantly improve depressive symptoms** in teenagers.

Ways to Cope with Depression: (Page 103 in *The RGP: Student Edition*)

1. Connect with others.
2. Practice Self-Care.
3. Challenge and replace negative thoughts with positive and self-compassionate ideas.

Brain Power (Page 104 in *The RGP: Student Edition*)

With the onset of adolescent depression linked to a ==hormonal mechanism== (Patton et al., 1996), adolescence is a critical time when stressors during this sensitive brain development period can cause brain malfunctions (i.e., ten- to eleven-year-old children exhibiting ==Amygdala damage due to abuse==) (Pechel et al., 2014).

In a 1,100-participant study of patients diagnosed with depression, fMRI scans were taken, and researchers noted similarities in the brain and categorized their depressive symptoms into four biotypes: the Insula, **Orbitofrontal Cortex**, Ventromedial Prefrontal Cortex, and multiple subcortical areas (i.e., **Corpus Callosum**, **Hippocampal**, Amygdala, Thalamus, and Putamen).

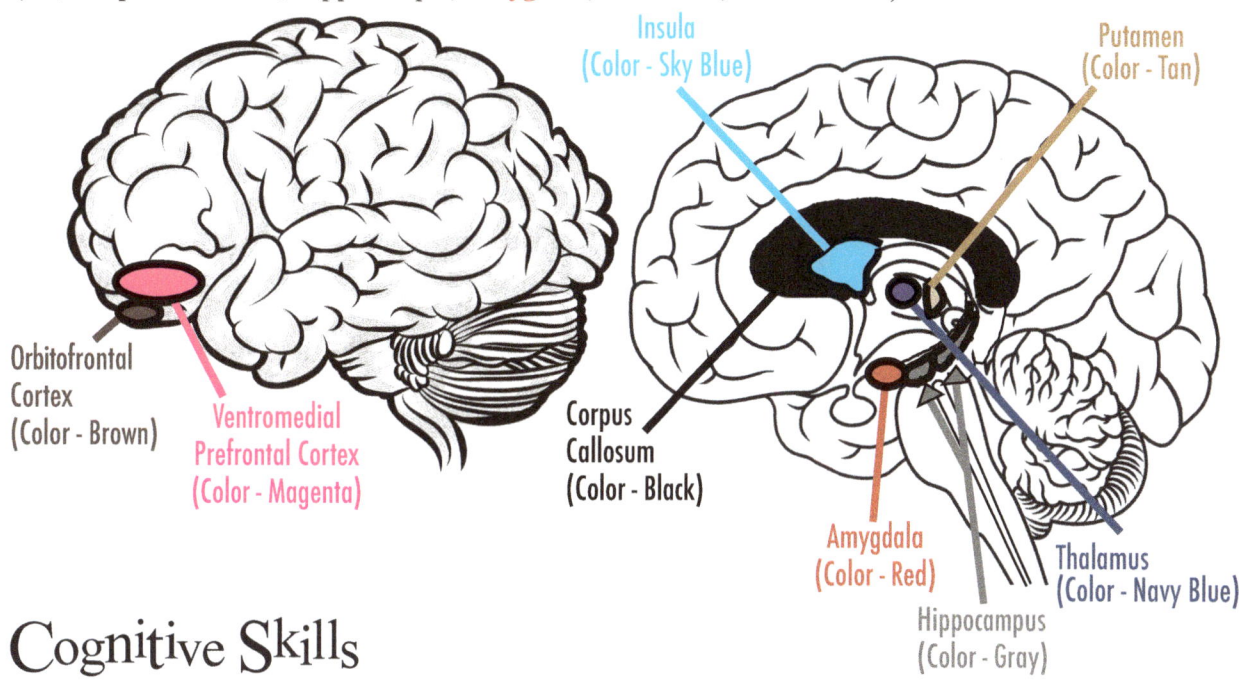

Cognitive Skills

- **Talking Points for Cognitive Skills Section:** (Page 105 in *The RGP: Student Edition*)

Step #2: Gauging Your Feelings

Possible Social Depression Feelings:

10. Extreme anxiety/I'm having a panic attack—can't be social.
9. Very anxious/My heart is racing. I feel I have no friends.
8. High anxiety/I feel distressed and want to stay home.
7. Moderate-to-high anxiety/I feel overwhelmed and lonely.
6. Moderately anxious/I don't want to talk to anyone.
5. Mild-to-moderate anxiety/Who would want to be my friend?
4. Mild anxiety/I have a lot of self doubt—feeling down.
3. Minimal anxiety/I have some self doubt—feeling down.
2. Feeling good/I feel happy most of the time.
1. No anxiety/I am extremely happy all the time.

Step #3: Overcoming Obstacles

Ideas on Social Depression Fears:

10. Everyday I'll get outside and keep social connections.
9. I'll get outside, get grounded, and do yoga with a friend.
8. I will work on building a social calendar to get me outside.
7. I will do breathing exercise to bring me peace and calmness.
6. I will practice "I am" statements to increase my confidence.
5. I will build a support system of people who care about me.
4. I'll build self-compassion writing one thing I like about myself.
3. I will watch online videos with tips on overcoming depression.
2. I will watch a movie about a person who is depressed.
1. I will listen to an upbeat song about feeling down.

If you are experiencing an emergency, please seek immediate assistance from a parent/guardian, school counselor, teacher, or medical professional or call 911.

This book is sold with the understanding that the publisher and the author are not engaged in rendering medical, legal, or other professional advice or services.
If professional assistance is required, the services of a competent professional should be sought.

• Self-Harm •

> **FOR LESSON PLANNING PURPOSES - AMOUNT OF TIME TO ALLOCATE: 35 minutes**
> *Add 4 minutes to take the Reflections Publishing Communication Assessment/Add time to the Mindfulness section (if possible), as 20 minutes provides optimal benefits.
>
> - 4114U and Student Activity - 7 minutes PLUS Class Discussion - 15 minutes
> - Playbook Strategy #1: Understanding Brain Power - 1 minute
> - Playbook Strategy #2: Learning Cognitive Strategies - 10 minutes
>   - Step #1 Expressive Writing - 2 minutes
>   - Step #2: Gauging Your Feelings - 4 minutes
>   - Step #3 Overcoming Obstacles - 4 minutes
> - Playbook Strategy #3: Learning Communication Strategies - 3 minutes
>   - *Reflections Publishing Communication Assessment - 4 minutes
> - Playbook Strategy #4: Learning Mindfulness Strategies - 3 minutes
> - Playbook Strategy #5: Developing New Habits - 2 minutes
> - Playbook Strategy #6: Anxiety-Buster To-Do List - 1 minute

• Facilitator Talking Points: (Page 108 in *The RGP: Student Edition*)

- At an alarming rate, adolescents with self-injurious thoughts and behaviors (SITBs) are tragically on an upward trend (Nock et al, 2019). Many people consider self-harm and nonsuicidal self-injury (NSSI) a current crisis (Wester, Wachter Morris, & Williams, 2017).
- Even going back two thousand years ago, Aristotle described Greek teenagers as "passionate, irascible, and apt to be carried away by their impulses" (Jensen & Ellis Nutt, 2015).
- Teenagers act impulsively and are vulnerable to the power of suggestion because during their formative brain development years, their brain gets "more of a sense of reward than an adult brain."
- The adolescent brain is in a sensitive state and gets splashed with more dopamine in "sensation-seeking situations" than an adult brain (Jensen & Ellis Nutt, 2015).
- In a Dartmouth College study, scientists noted in an fMRI experience exactly why and how this happens in the teenage brain. Going back to puberty, the Frontal Cortex in the teen brain is still wiring itself together, thus making it difficult for teens to understand any consequences of their actions, as well as accurately assess risks and rewards (Reyna & Frank, 2006).
- The study described this thought process of costs versus benefits as moving slower in their brain versus an adult's brain. An adolescent brain focuses more on the "reason" they might want to do something versus the consequence of their decision because the areas around their Frontal Lobe are not fully connected and wired together yet (Reyna & Frank, 2006).
- An adult brain's Anterior Cingulate Cortex is fully developed, so the adult brain understands they are about to make a mistake and immediately process not to go through with the action (Steinberg, 2008).
- While students may think their bad choices are not their fault (i.e., due to their Frontal Cortex still developing), they learned the difference between right and wrong at the age of five. Plus, **when drugs and alcohol are added into the mix, all bets are off because they may cause an adolescent brain to wire incorrectly, and their brain may not function properly**.
- Research indicates that if students can have a game plan in place when they are struggling with resisting "sensation-seeking situations" and can redirect their attention and focus to something else, then research states that **self-harm ideation can pass in fifteen minutes**.
- Students need help creating a game plan to start training their brains to redirect those negative "sensation-seeking temptations" into positive thoughts and actions.
- **There has not been a person who attempted self-harm and survived who wished their attempt was successful**. In fact, every person interviewed revealed **they immediately regretted their decision—realizing what they thought was so horrible was not that bad, and they did not want to die**.

• Self-Harm Student Activity: (Page 109 in *The RGP: Student Edition*)

Ideas to help adolescents get through 15 minutes of self-harm ideation.

Brain Power (Page 110 in *The RGP: Student Edition*)

The **Anterior Cingular Cortex** (which works as a behavior monitor to help identify mistakes) is not fully wired in the adolescent, developing brain; thus, they react impulsively and passionately and cannot process and make good decisions (Jensen & Ellis Nut, 2015). Between adolescence and adulthood, the self-regulation and cognitive control systems mature; thus, your impulsive sensation-seeking and risk-taking behaviors decline as your **Lateral Prefrontal Cortex**, **Parietal Cortex**, and **Anterior Cingular Cortex** are wired together (Steinberg, 2008).

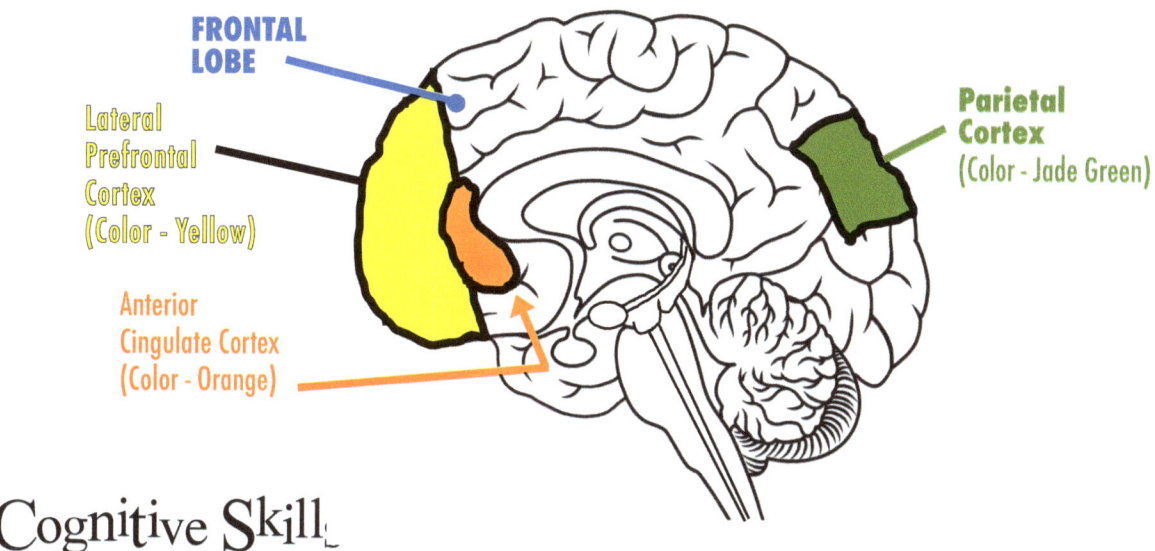

Cognitive Skills

- **Talking Points for Cognitive Skills Section:** (Page 111 in *The RGP: Student Edition*)

Step #2: Gauging Your Feelings

How you May Feel About Self-Harm:

10. Extreme anxiety/I need to seek help immediately.
9. Very anxious/My heart is racing.
8. High anxiety/I don't want to continue feeling like this.
7. Moderate-to-high anxiety/I am afraid to be by myself.
6. Moderately anxious/I don't want to be around anyone.
5. Mild-to-moderate anxiety/I feel like life is too hard.
4. Mild anxiety/I feel better pinching myself.
3. Minimal anxiety/I feel better picking at my nails.
2. Feeling good/I feel good and don't understand self-harm.
1. No anxiety/I love myself and would never hurt myself.

Step #3: Overcoming Obstacles

Ideas on Overcoming Self-Harm Fears:

10. I am confident with no intentions of harming myself.
9. I will help someone else who is struggling with self-harm.
8. I will journal why I ever wanted to commit self-harm.
7. I will do the breathing exercise to help overcome self-harm.
6. I will practice "I am" statements to overcome self-harm.
5. I will join a group self-harm therapy group.
4. I will stay away from friends who self-harm.
3. I will watch a movie about self-harm.
2. I will watch a television show about teen self-harm.
1. I will listen to a song about self-harm.

Key Takeaway

- **Suicide Hot line: 988**

If you are experiencing an emergency, please seek immediate assistance from a parent/guardian, school counselor, teacher, or medical professional or call 911 or 988.

This book is sold with the understanding that the publisher and the author are not engaged in rendering medical, legal, or other professional advice or services. If professional assistance is required, the services of a competent professional should be sought.

• Substance Abuse - Alcohol & Drugs •

> **FOR LESSON PLANNING PURPOSES - AMOUNT OF TIME TO ALLOCATE: 35 minutes**
> *Add 4 minutes to take the Reflections Publishing Communication Assessment/Add time to the Mindfulness section (if possible), as 20 minutes provides optimal benefits.
>
> - 4114U and Student Activity - 7 minutes PLUS Class Discussion - 15 minutes
> - Playbook Strategy #1: Understanding Brain Power - 3 minutes
> - Playbook Strategy #2: Learning Cognitive Strategies - 10 minutes
>   - Step #1 Expressive Writing - 2 minutes
>   - Step #2: Gauging Your Feelings - 4 minutes
>   - Step #3 Overcoming Obstacles - 4 minutes
> - Playbook Strategy #3: Learning Communication Strategies - 2 minutes
>   - *Reflections Publishing Communication Assessment - 4 minutes
> - Playbook Strategy #4: Learning Mindfulness Strategies - 2 minutes
> - Playbook Strategy #5: Developing New Habits - 2 minutes
> - Playbook Strategy #6: Anxiety-Buster To-Do List - 1 minute

- **Facilitator Talking Points:** (Page 114 in *The RGP: Student Edition*)
  - **Student Instructions:** Get a yellow highlighter and mark the sentences discussing what happens to the developing brain when drugs and alcohol are consumed daily. After reading the text, discuss as a class.
  - Have students see the research for themselves and go to their web browser to type the following keywords: (adolescent) AND (cannabis) AND (fMRI) AND (schizophrenia)

- **Two Rules: 1. Make Good Choices and 2. Use Common Sense**
- Teens with no family history are developing schizophrenia due to their daily cannabis use. Now a pandemic, Harvard instructor started teaching a class on this subject.
- While your brain is "plastic" and "livewired," the consumption of weed and some other drugs on a daily basis, while your Prefrontal Cortex is developing, may damage your brain to a point of no return.
- According to the United Nations Office on Drugs and Crime (UNODC), two-thirds of the data reported from participating countries rank cannabis as its primary substance abuse.
- With weed legalized in some states, adolescents now view weed the same as watching their parents drink alcohol. Weed is getting normalized, with kids saying, "It relaxes me."
- Students have no idea **the formulation they are intaking**.
- Adolescence is a known time when your brain properly wires its fiber tracts—connecting your cognitive, motor, and sensory functions (Paus et al., 1999).
- The law of no alcohol or drugs until the age of 21 is because students can damage their developing brains. Harvard Medical School reports that the brain may develop until age 30 (2022, January 31).
- **Some individuals are at even more risk of adverse effects of consuming weed—developing symptoms of psychotic illness, cognitive impairment, and long-term addiction** (Curran et al., 2016). The Koob and Volkow Model of Addiction explains how the three stages of weed addiction affect three major neurocircuits in the brain.
- In a study conducted in New Zealand, individuals who developed a weed addiction during their adolescent years **reported a decline of up to six IQ points**. Another study links cognitive changes to weed consumption with a **decline of eight points** (Meier et al., 2012).
- Weed contains 100 unique ingredients called cannabinoids, and the two most prominent ingredients are Delta9-tetrahydrocannabinol (Δ^9-THC) and cannabidiol (CBD), which tend to have adverse effects on the developing human brain behavior. Research indicates that Δ^9-THC impairs learning, produces psychosis-like effects and increases anxiety (Curran et al., 2016).
- Share the story of a teenager who smoked weed in a vape pen that was also laced with a horse tranquilizer. This person almost died, but fortunately, **one of the teenagers had some common sense and knew they were protected by The Good Samaritan Law and called 911**.
- Bossong & Niesink, (2010) believed that abnormal pruning likely occurs when the toxic THC enters the brain during the critical time of maturation—affecting the synaptic pruning in the cerebellum (Casu et al., 2005) and prefrontal cortex (Bossong & Niesink, 2010).

Brain Power (Page 116 in *The RGP: Student Edition*)

Positron emission tomography (PET) scans show proof that adolescents who heavily and regularly consume weed during their key formative brain development years (i.e., puberty through at least the age of 25-years-old), show a reduction in the **Striatal Dopamine Synthesis**; these individuals are labeled with the term "amotivation syndrome". In a post-mortem study by Rapp et al. (2012), cannabis use is linked to volume loss in the brain—in the **Cingulum**, the **Dorsolateral Prefrontal Cortex**, and the **Cerebellum**.

In a study by Meier et al. (2012) of 1,037 individuals, daily cannabis use was studied beginning with a neuropsychological test when the participants were 13-years-old. Interviews with these same participants occurred at ages 18-, 21-, 26-, 32-, and 38-years-old. The findings prove a significant lifetime, neurotoxic effect on kids who start using weed in their teens.

At one point, weed was considered to be harmless; however, research indicates through long-term studies that when weed consumption begins during the formative brain development years (i.e., puberty through at least the age of 25-years-old) and used on a regular basis, weed is linked to severe weed dependence, a gateway to other drugs, lung disease, memory impairment, altering psychosocial development, poor cognitive performance, and mental health problems (i.e., schizophrenia and bipolar disorder).

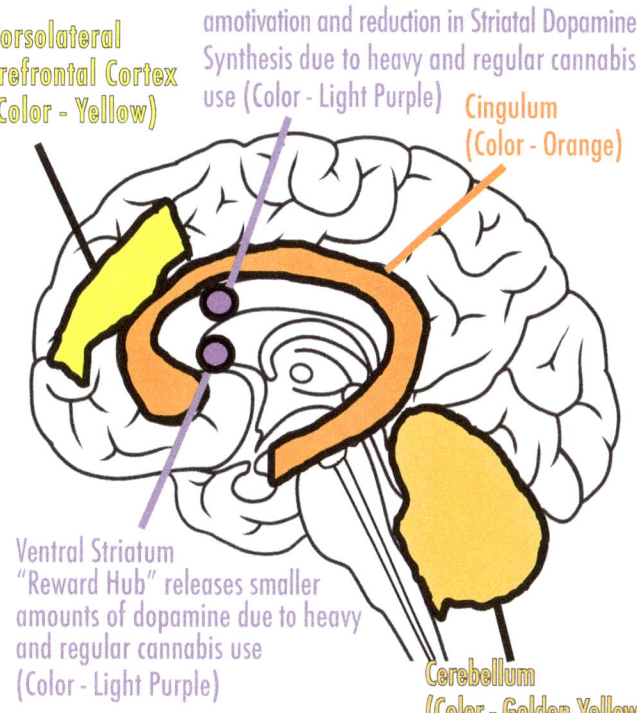

Dorsolateral Prefrontal Cortex (Color - Yellow)

Dorsal Striatum "Habit Hub" is tied to amotivation and reduction in Striatal Dopamine Synthesis due to heavy and regular cannabis use (Color - Light Purple)

Cingulum (Color - Orange)

Ventral Striatum "Reward Hub" releases smaller amounts of dopamine due to heavy and regular cannabis use (Color - Light Purple)

Cerebellum (Color - Golden Yellow)

Cognitive Skills

- **Talking Points for Cognitive Skills Section:** (Page 117 in *The RGP: Student Edition*)

Step #2: Gauging Your Feelings

How you May Feel About Drugs and Alcohol:

10. Extreme anxiety/I can't say, "NO!"
9. Very anxious/People keep pressuring me to try weed.
8. High anxiety/My heart is racing with the pressure.
7. Moderate-to-high anxiety/I feel overwhelmed with pressure.
6. Moderately anxious/Remember people pressuring me.
5. Mild-to-moderate anxiety/People won't leave me alone.
4. Mild anxiety/I feel judged that I am not doing drugs.
3. Minimal anxiety/I can see myself getting off track with drugs.
2. Feel good/I feel I can go into social situations saying, "NO!"
1. No anxiety/I feel confident in myself; I do not use drugs.

Step #3: Overcoming Obstacles

Ideas on Overcoming Drug and Alcohol Use:

10. I am confident I can now say, "NO!"
9. I will practice saying, "NO!" utilizing role playing scripts.
8. I will create a list of "Go-to Phrases" to avoid drugs.
7. I will do breathing exercises to help me relax and refocus.
6. I will practice "I am" statements to increase my confidence.
5. I will hang out with new friends who don't pressure me.
4. I will join group therapy, making new friends who support me.
3. I will watch online videos regarding damage of drug use.
2. I will watch a movie about overcoming drug use.
1. I will listen to an upbeat song about overcoming drug use.

If you are experiencing an emergency, please seek immediate assistance from a parent/guardian, school counselor, teacher, or medical professional or call 911.

This book is sold with the understanding that the publisher and the author are not engaged in rendering medical, legal, or other professional advice or services. If professional assistance is required, the services of a competent professional should be sought.

Section Nine

What's Your Game Plan?

Relationships

(Page 121 in *The RGP: Student Edition*)

LIFE TOPICS:

- Bullying/Cyberbullying - 122
- Caregiver - 128
- Friendships - 134
- Peer Pressure - 140

*Student Edition Pages

• Bullying and Cyberbullying •

> **FOR LESSON PLANNING PURPOSES - AMOUNT OF TIME TO ALLOCATE: 35 minutes**
> *Add 4 minutes to take the Reflections Publishing Communication Assessment/Add time to the Mindfulness section (if possible), as 20 minutes provides optimal benefits.
> - 4114U and Student Activity - 4 minutes PLUS Class Discussion - 10 minutes
> - Playbook Strategy #1: Understanding Brain Power - 6 minutes
> - Playbook Strategy #2: Learning Cognitive Strategies - 10 minutes
>   - Step #1 Expressive Writing - 2 minutes
>   - Step #2: Gauging Your Feelings - 4 minutes
>   - Step #3 Overcoming Obstacles - 4 minutes
> - Playbook Strategy #3: Learning Communication Strategies - 4 minutes
>   - *Reflections Publishing Communication Assessment - 4 minutes
> - Playbook Strategy #4: Learning Mindfulness Strategies - 2 minutes
> - Playbook Strategy #5: Developing New Habits - 2 minutes
> - Playbook Strategy #6: Anxiety-Buster To-Do List - 1 minute

• Facilitator Talking Points: (Page 122 in *The RGP: Student Edition*)

- Bullying is a one-sided act of peer abuse that occurs to another, normally innocent person. While calling the act peer abuse might sound extreme, but this terminology is more representative of when one person is mean to another human being—for absolutely no reason.
- One of the most challenging concepts for any person to process who receives bullying behavior is that someone would treat them in a way they would never consider treating someone else.
- A perpetrator might be mean to someone because they are:
  1. Extremely insecure. Happy and content people do not feel the need to put others down.
  2. Low in self-confidence. Around third grade, students start to notice and compare themselves to classmates. In some circumstances, this is the age when students start to struggle in school, so to compensate for this insecurity, aggressors start picking on classmates who are good students.
  3. Jealous. This is, unfortunately an insecurity and habit that some parents pass down to their children; it is a learned behavior.
- Expert Alison Trachtman Hill in the *Face 2 Face* book encourages people not to call a fellow teenager a bully but to instead label the behavior instead of the person. She states, **"kids are not good or bad—they make good or bad decisions."** Additionally, she divides the social aspect of peer abuse into the following three roles:

  - **• The Aggressor:**   This person executes the bad, peer abuse behavior.
  - **• The Target:**   This person receives the peer abuse.
  - **• The Witness:**   This person is called a "Witness" and not a "Bystander" because if you **witness someone getting picked on, you have a responsibility to report it** to an adult or authority figure.

• How to Create a Peer Abuse Shield Student Activity: (Page 123 in *The RGP: Student Edition*)
Help students build a shield of defense armor to combat an aggressor's attack:
- Stand tall with your head held high.
- Talk in a strong, confident, and firm voice.
- Look the aggressor in the eye when you talk.
- Let the aggressor's comments bounce off your shield. Don't let their words enter your head or heart.
- Try not to react to aggressors. A reaction may be exactly what they are looking to provoke. Breathe deeply and remove yourself from the situation as quickly as possible.
- If you stay with a group of friends, aggressors will be less likely to target you.

Brain Power (Page 124 in *The RGP: Student Edition*)

According to Adams, Sanko, & Bukowski (2011), just the presence of a best friend can serve as a protective buffer against the negative effect of a bad experience on an individual's global self-worth, as well as altercations created in the **Hypothalamic-Pituitary-Adrenocortical (HPA) axis**—due to less cortisol released. **Have students use a web search engine to find the location of the HPA axis in their brain, and then, in the space below, draw their own version of a brain labeling the HPA axis in their illustration.**

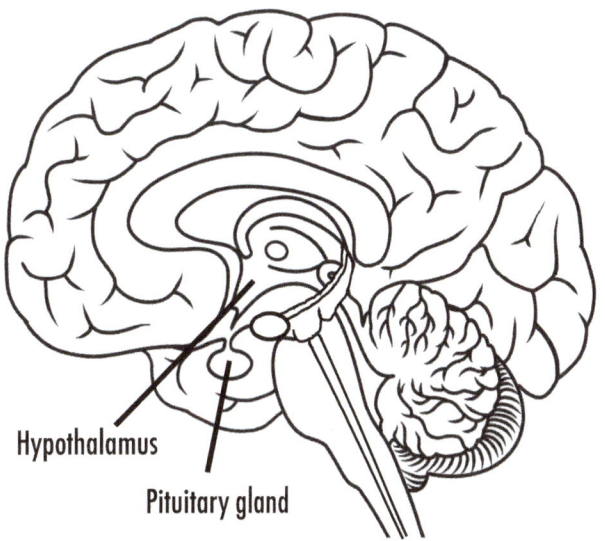

Hypothalamus
Pituitary gland

Cognitive Skills

• **Talking Points for Cognitive Skills Section:** (Page 125 in *The RGP: Student Edition*)

Step #2: Gauging Your Feelings

How you May Feel About Getting Bullied:

10. Extreme anxiety/Experiencing severe suffering from peer abuse.
9. Very anxious/Having a panic attack—feel powerless.
8. High anxiety/I don't see the bullying ever stopping.
7. Moderate-to-high anxiety/I'm afraid what the bully will do to me.
6. Moderately anxious/I feel humiliated from bullying.
5. Mild-to-moderate anxiety/I feel out of control when bullied.
4. Mild anxiety/This bully is affecting my well-being.
3. Minimal anxiety/I feel like I might be the target of a bully.
2. Feeling good/I am aware that people get bullied.
1. No anxiety/I have never experienced a bullying situation.

Step #3: Overcoming Obstacles

Ideas on Overcoming Bullying Fears:

10. I am confident to study up to bullies and support others too.
9. I will rehearse with role-playing scripts to respond to bullying.
8. I will create coping strategies so I am prepared for bullying.
7. I will practice breathing exercises to not let bully affect me.
6. I will build self-esteem with practicing "I am" statements.
5. I will run an anti-bullying club at my school.
4. I will join a bullying support group and seek help from teachers.
3. I will watch online videos and TikToks on bullying.
2. I will watch a movie about a student getting bullied.
1. I will listen to an upbeat song about overcoming bullying.

Students' Key Takeaway

If you are a victim of cyberbullying, there are steps you can take to shut down the abuse. The first step is to document and log the abuse so you can validate your case. The second step is to then report this abuse to a parent/guardian and/or school official.

If you are experiencing an emergency, please seek immediate assistance from a parent/guardian, school counselor, teacher, or medical professional or call 911.
This book is sold with the understanding that the publisher and the author are not engaged in rendering medical, legal, or other professional advice or services.
If professional assistance is required, the services of a competent professional should be sought.

• Caregiver •

> **FOR LESSON PLANNING PURPOSES - AMOUNT OF TIME TO ALLOCATE: 25 minutes**
> *Add 4 minutes to take the Reflections Publishing Communication Assessment/Add time to the Mindfulness section (if possible), as 20 minutes provides optimal benefits.
>
> - 4114U and Student Activity - 4 minutes PLUS Class Discussion - 7 minutes
> - Playbook Strategy #1: Understanding Brain Power - 1 minute
> - Playbook Strategy #2: Learning Cognitive Strategies - 10 minutes
>   - Step #1 Expressive Writing - 2 minutes
>   - Step #2 Gauging Your Feelings - 4 minutes
>   - Step #3 Overcoming Obstacles - 4 minutes
> - Playbook Strategy #3: Learning Communication Strategies - 2 minutes
>   - *Reflections Publishing Communication Assessment - 4 minutes
> - Playbook Strategy #4: Learning Mindfulness Strategies - 2 minutes
> - Playbook Strategy #5: Developing New Habits - 2 minutes
> - Playbook Strategy #6: Anxiety-Buster To-Do List - 1 minute

• Facilitator Talking Points: (Page 128 in *The RGP: Student Edition*)

- Family dynamics are quite interesting, and as the phrases go—"we all are products of our childhood" and "the apple doesn't fall far from the tree;" these phrases are so true.
- What your student considers to be a normal family is how they see their own family communicate and operate throughout their childhood.
- If people in their family yell and argue, they will likely think that behavior is normal.
- This is why individuals who are abused as children continue the cycle of abuse onto their own children.

• Communication from the Caregive (Parent/Guardian) Perspective:

From a parent/guardian perspective, humans have a limited energy supply. Just like an electric car getting plugged into an electrical outlet, it gains the energy it needs to operate. The human body does the same thing, except we go to sleep to restore and gain energy for the next day. Just like some electric cars, it has a gas option, and humans can supplement caffeine or exercise to give them a boost; however, if we push too hard, our bodies can break down like a car. When we communicate with people effectively, we use less energy and have more of a reserve to spend that energy elsewhere. If relations within the family network are positive, then the energy supply is slowly used and can even be restored and regenerated together. When children know they are loved unconditionally, it creates a workable framework of communication that allows parents to walk alongside them as they grow up and the family network to function in a healthy manner.

• Communication from the Student's Perspective:

When students feel they can talk to people without feeling judged, disrespected, or guilty, they will open up to you. When communicating with people, consider how self-complex a person is and the timing of the communication with them. "Pick your moments" and recognize that when you care about somebody, you do not intentionally push their buttons.

• Creating Family Connections:

Why is it so hard to praise the ones we care about the most? Communication becomes fuzzy when we are too busy, too tired, or possibly not wanting to listen to the opinions of friends, family, classmates, or coworkers. When we communicate with each other in the method that fills our energy and love tanks, we can function to our full potential - as an individual, a parent, a spouse, a child, a classmate, a coworker, etc.

• Caregiver (Parent/Guardian) Relations Activity (Page 129 in *The RGP: Student Edition*)

Have students read through the anonymous student comments shared on **page 129** of the Reflections Publishing Communication Assessment. Discuss ways students could try to improve these communication struggles.

Brain Power (Page 130 in *The RGP: Student Edition*)

According to Platek et al. (2009), when comparing family faces to friend faces, the **Posterior Cingulate** and **Cuneus** are activated in the brain. Also, familiar family faces activate the Anterior Medial Substrates (**Anterior Cingulate Cortex** and **Medial Prefrontal Cortex**) areas in the brain.

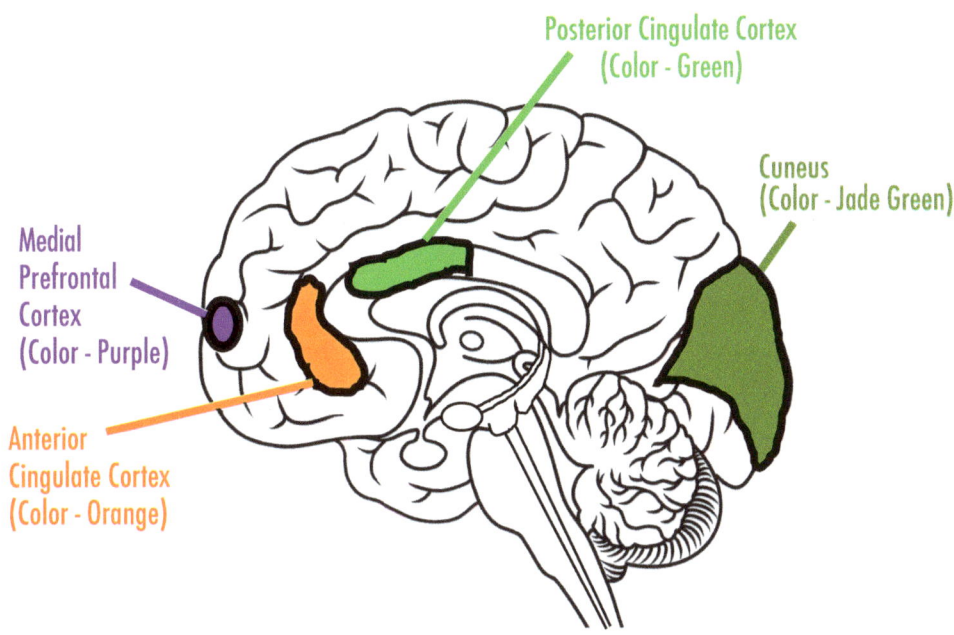

Cognitive Skills

- **Talking Points for Cognitive Skills Section:** (Page 131 in *The RGP: Student Edition*)

Step #2: Gauging Your Feelings

How You May Feel About Your Family:

10. Extreme anxiety/I'm afraid my parents will yell at me.
9. Very anxious/My heart's racing thinking of my dad's reaction.
8. High anxiety/I don't feel like I can talk to my parents.
7. Moderate-to-high anxiety/I feel overwhelmed with emotion.
6. Moderately anxious/I am scared to talk to my family.
5. Mild-to-moderate anxiety/I am grateful I can talk to my mom.
4. Mild anxiety/My thoughts spiral when I try talking to my dad.
3. Minimal anxiety/I feel nervous talking to my dad.
2. Feeling good/I feel like I can talk to my parents.
1. No anxiety/I feel I can to talk to my parents about anything.

Step #3: Overcoming Obstacles

Thoughts on Overcoming Family Fears:

10. I am confident to talk to my parents.
9. I will practice things to say to my parents.
8. I will journal ideas on how to express how I feel.
7. I will do breathing exercises to help me relax.
6. I will practice "I am" statements to increase my confidence.
5. I will work with a counselor to help give me pointers.
4. I will join a study group and identify what I still need to learn.
3. I will watch online videos with lessons about famiy drama.
2. I will watch a movie about family vacations.
1. I will listen to an upbeat song about loving families.

If any information in this playbook is upsetting, please talk to a parent/guardian, school counselor, teacher, or medical professional.
This book is sold with the understanding that the publisher and the author are not engaged in rendering medical, legal, or other professional advice or services.
If professional assistance is required, the services of a competent professional should be sought.

• Friendships •

> **FOR LESSON PLANNING PURPOSES - AMOUNT OF TIME TO ALLOCATE: 25 minutes**
> *Add 4 minutes to take the Reflections Publishing Communication Assessment/Add time to the Mindfulness section (if possible), as 20 minutes provides optimal benefits.
> - 4II4U, Friendship Bucket Activity, & Friendship Checklist - 5 minutes/ Class Discussion - 7 minutes
> - Playbook Strategy #1: Understanding Brain Power - 1 minute
> - Playbook Strategy #2: Learning Cognitive Strategies - 10 minutes
>   - Step #1 Expressive Writing - 2 minutes
>   - Step #2: Gauging Your Feelings - 4 minutes
>   - Step #3 Overcoming Obstacles - 4 minutes
> - Playbook Strategy #3: Learning Communication Strategies - 1 minute
>   - *Reflections Publishing Communication Assessment - 4 minutes
> - Playbook Strategy #4: Learning Mindfulness Strategies - 3 minutes
> - Playbook Strategy #5: Developing New Habits - 2 minutes
> - Playbook Strategy #6: Anxiety-Buster To-Do List - 1 minute

• Facilitator Talking Points: (Page 134 in *The RGP: Student Edition*)

4II4U for Your Students: Having one loyal friend provides a resistance and buffer to life stressors

Friendship Bucket Activity Instructions: (Pages 134-135 in *The RGP: Student Edition*)

If students can learn to identify their friends as "24/7 Friends," "Common Interest Friends, "Friends for a Season," or "Peer Pressure Friends," then they know where to invest their time and energy in friendships. Inform them it is okay to be friends with someone for "Just a Season." People come and go in our lives for a purpose or life lesson. While it may hurt when a friendship fizzles, it is okay to classify a person as a "Friend for a Season." Have your learners think about their group of friends and put them into one of the following buckets:

"24/7 Friend" Bucket
- I can share and trust intimate thoughts and feelings with this person.
- This individual is always a loyal, reliable, trustworthy friend—24 hours a day, 7 days a week.
- This person has a positive influence on me.
- I feel good about myself after spending time with this friend.
- This friend is happy for me when good things come my way.

"Common Interest Friend" Bucket
- I enjoy this person's company, but we do not share secrets or intimate thoughts and feelings.
- This friend is someone you likely met playing on the same sports team or extracurricular activity.

"Friend for a Season" Bucket
- I used to be really close friends, but have grown apart.
- I continue to have a friendly relationship with them.

"Peer Pressure Friend" Bucket
- This person has gotten you to do things you know are not morally correct.
- This individual encourages you to exclude others.

Make Their Own Category

Brain Power (Page 136 in *The RGP: Student Edition*)

According to Becht et al. (2020), having just one good, reliable friend can provide a buffer of protection in your student's brain. Having a childhood best friend instills developmental resilience in adolescents, allowing them to achieve their goals and develop strong social connections with their peers. Supportive friendships lead to more resilient brain functioning, which is highlighted below—affecting their neurodevelopmental trajectories within the social-cognitive realm.

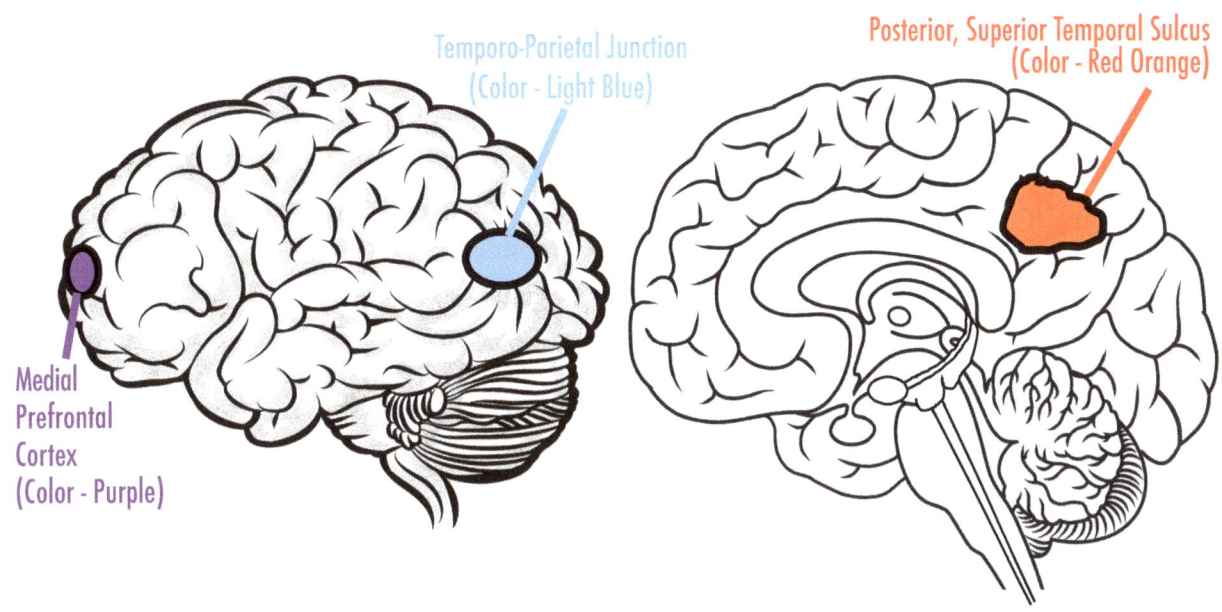

Temporo-Parietal Junction (Color - Light Blue)

Posterior, Superior Temporal Sulcus (Color - Red Orange)

Medial Prefrontal Cortex (Color - Purple)

Cognitive Skills

• **Talking Points for Cognitive Skills Section:** (Page 137 in *The RGP: Student Edition*)

Step #2: Gauging Your Feelings

How you May Feel About Friendships:

10. Extreme anxiety/I don't think anyone is my friend.
9. Very anxious/I don't think I have any true friends.
8. High anxiety/My heart is racing because I don't trust people.
7. Moderate-to-high anxiety/I feel people judge me.
6. Moderately anxious/I think people are critiquing me.
5. Mild-to-moderate anxiety/I ruminate social situations.
4. Mild anxiety/ I am pretty sure my friends are trustworthy.
3. Minimal anxiety/ I feel pretty confident in my friendships.
2. Feeling good/ I feel confident in my friendships.
1. No anxiety/I think everyone is my friend.

Step #3: Overcoming Obstacles

Overcoming Fear of New Friendships:

10. I will attend the end-of-year party for my grade.
9. I will share some personal information with a new friend.
8. I will meet a friend for coffee before school.
7. I will start a study group with some potential new friends.
6. I will ask someone in math class a homework question.
5. I will ask a new person to be my partner at practice warm-up.
4. I will say hello to everyone at school.
3. I will watch online videos about friendship.
2. I will watch a movie about middle/high school friendships.
1. I will listen to an upbeat song about friendship.

If any information in this playbook is upsetting, please talk to a parent/guardian, school counselor, teacher, or medical professional.
This book is sold with the understanding that the publisher and the author are not engaged in rendering medical, legal, or other professional advice or services.
If professional assistance is required, the services of a competent professional should be sought.

• Peer Pressure •

> **FOR LESSON PLANNING PURPOSES - AMOUNT OF TIME TO ALLOCATE: 30 minutes**
> *Add 4 minutes to take the Reflections Publishing Communication Assessment/Add time to the Mindfulness section (if possible), as 20 minutes provides optimal benefits.
>
> - 4114U and Student Activity - 6 minutes PLUS Class Discussion - 10 minutes
> - Playbook Strategy #1: Understanding Brain Power - 1 minute
> - Playbook Strategy #2: Learning Cognitive Strategies - 10 minutes
>   - Step #1 Expressive Writing - 2 minutes
>   - Step #2 Gauging Your Feelings - 4 minutes
>   - Step #3 Overcoming Obstacles - 4 minutes
> - Playbook Strategy #3: Learning Communication Strategies - 3 minutes
>   - *Reflections Publishing Communication Assessment - 4 minutes
> - Playbook Strategy #4: Learning Mindfulness Strategies - 3 minutes
> - Playbook Strategy #5: Developing New Habits - 2 minutes
> - Playbook Strategy #6: Anxiety-Buster To-Do List - 1 minute

• Facilitator Talking Points: (Page 140 in *The RGP: Student Edition*)

- Peer pressure is a challenge for all teenagers, and this section will reiterate and incorporate concepts discussed in the "What's Your Legacy? - Core Values" section.
- Everyone deals with peer pressure at some point in their life; it tests a person's core beliefs and values.
- One of the best ways to combat peer pressure is for students to work on building up their self-esteem and confidence. Teenagers who typically cave into peer pressure have low self-esteem and a tendency to do or say anything to fit into their peer group.

Here are some things to discuss with students when they struggle to stand up for themselves, especially when someone is trying to get them to do something they know is wrong.

1. If you know your core values and have a strong belief system, then it makes it easier to say "no" in pressure situations. Focusing on creating a solid sense of self and knowing who you are and what you stand for makes it much easier to say "no."
2. Have a game plan in place so when people try to get you to do something unwanted, then you can have a witty comeback that redirects your entire friend group to a more desired activity.
3. Choose your friends carefully. People who are your true friends will not try to force you to do something that you do not want to do.
4. Make decisions and choices that you will not regret later. Ask any adult and they can tell you stories about classmates who made poor decisions. A bad choice or decision lasts a lifetime, and do not let anyone convince you otherwise.
5. Stay in a safe environment that will not place you in a possible bad situation.
6. A friend who has your back 24 hours a day/7 days a week (a 24/7 friend) will always support you and your morals. Their values will align with your own, so you never have to defend yourself. A true and loyal friend will always support and respect your choices and understand that your choices and decisions have a consequence for any action you perform.

• Peer Pressure Student Activity: (Page 141 in *The RGP: Student Edition*)

- **List all of the ways you have experienced peer pressure:**
- **Doodle or Draw how you feel when you experience peer pressure:**

• Communication Skills Student Activity: (Page 144 in *The RGP: Student Edition*)

- Have students practice write their own "Go-To Phrase" to stand up for themselves.

Brain Power (Page 142 in *The RGP: Student Edition*)

The influence of peer feedback and peer pressure on how a person should think shows up in activated clusters in the **Ventrolateral Prefrontal Cortex**, **Medial Prefrontal Cortex**, **Superior Temporal Gyrus/Sulcus**, and **Occipital Cortex**.

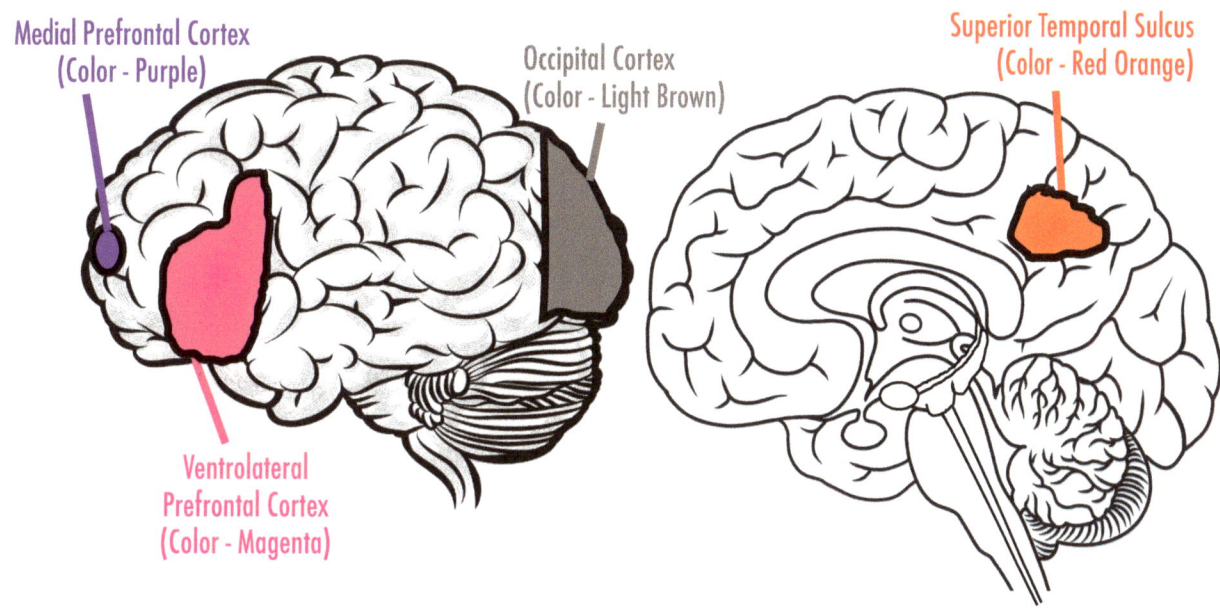

Medial Prefrontal Cortex (Color - Purple)
Occipital Cortex (Color - Light Brown)
Superior Temporal Sulcus (Color - Red Orange)
Ventrolateral Prefrontal Cortex (Color - Magenta)

Cognitive Skills

- **Talking Points for Cognitive Skills Section:** (Page 143 in *The RGP: Student Edition*)

Step #2: Gauging Your Feelings

Possible Ideas on Feeling Peer Pressure:

10. Extreme anxiety/I feel like I'm having a panic attack.
9. Very anxious/I am feeling emotional turmoil.
8. High anxiety/I feel overwhelmed by the pressure.
7. Moderate-to-high anxiety/I'm afraid of negative consequences.
6. Moderately anxious/Feeling pressure from peers to conform.
5. Mild-to-moderate anxiety/I'm uncomfortable: peer pressure.
4. Mild anxiety/I'm having trouble staying true to my values.
3. Minimal anxiety/I'm uneasy about possible peer pressure.
2. Feeling good/I am aware that peer pressure exists.
1. No anxiety/I haven't encountered a peer pressure situation.

Step #3: Overcoming Obstacles

Ideas on Overcoming Peer Pressure:

10. I am confident in handling peer pressure.
9. I will talk to my parents about helping with pressure.
8. I will do role playing for peer presssure.
7. I will do the breathing exercise that helps me to relax.
6. I will practice "I am" statements to increase my confidence.
5. I will work with a counselor to help with peer pressure.
4. I will join a study group and identify what I still need to learn.
3. I will watch online videos with lessons about peer pressure.
2. I will watch a movie about middle/high school pressure.
1. I will listen to an upbeat song about peer pressure.

If any information in this playbook is upsetting, please talk to a parent/guardian, school counselor, teacher, or medical professional.
This book is sold with the understanding that the publisher and the author are not engaged in rendering medical, legal, or other professional advice or services.
If professional assistance is required, the services of a competent professional should be sought.

Section Ten

The Resilience Game Plan Post-Assessment

(Page 147 in *The RGP: Student Edition*)

***Student Edition Pages**

• *The Resilience Game Plan* Post-Assessment •

- **STEP #1:** Take this Post-Assessment after completing *The Resilience Game Plan*.
- **STEP #2:** Rank your Subjective Well-Being (from 1-10) and then ***For every "Yes" response, write an "X" on the right-hand line.**

Subjective Well-Being: (Rank from 1-10)

1. How satisfied are you with your life? (1 Extremely Unsatisfied - to - 10 Extremely Satisfied) _____
2. What are your feelings about people or situations in your life? (1 Extreme Anxiety - to - 10 Extremely Peaceful) _____
3. Do you feel your life has meaning and purpose? (1 Extremely Disagree - to - 10 Extremely Agree) _____

WHAT'S YOUR GAME PLAN? • WARM-UP

Academic Pressures:

1. Do you feel you belong and are connected at your school?
   ☐ Yes - I belong to teams/clubs   ☐ No - I feel like an outsider   *** (If "Yes," write "X" here:)** _____
2. Do you find your schoolwork engaging and interesting?
   ☐ Yes - I am learning for the "love of learning"   ☐ No - I am a "robo-learner"/only learn for tests _____
3. Do you find your schoolwork meaningful and relevant to real life?
   ☐ Yes - I am learning life-long skills   ☐ No - I am a "robo-learner"/only learn for tests _____
4. Do you feel respected and valued at school?
   ☐ Yes   ☐ No _____
5. Do you have a close connection to at least one teacher at school?
   ☐ Yes - list name: _____   ☐ No _____

Habit Formation: New Habits and Breaking Old Habits:

1. Do you have habits you want to break? If Yes, list: _____ _____
2. Do you have new habits you want to form? If Yes, list: _____ _____

What's Your Legacy? Knowing Your Core Values:

1. How do you want to be remembered after you graduate? List: _____

Who Are Your Personal "Cheerleaders," Coaches, and/or Mentors:

1. Do you have a mentor/cheerleader in your life?
   ☐ Yes - list name: _____   ☐ No _____

WHAT'S YOUR GAME PLAN? • LIFE CHOICES

Self and Identity: List Your Peer Friend Group: _____

1. Do you associate your identity with your peer group? If "Yes," list your friend group on the line above and put "X" here: _____

Social Media:

1. Do you feel good about yourself after spending time on Social Media (e.g., Instragram, Snapchat, and TikTok)?
   ☐ Yes - I feel good about myself.   ☐ No - I feel worse about myself _____

Time Management - Life Balance:

1. Do you think you have a good life balance?
   ☐ Yes   ☐ Average   ☐ No _____

WHAT'S YOUR GAME PLAN? • LIFE CRISES

Abuse - Domestic, Physical, and Verbal:

1. Do you have a concern of feeling unsafe at school and home?
   ☐ Yes - List location: _____ ☐ No _____

2. Do you feel anxious at home (i.e., not enough food or do not feel protected)?
   ☐ Yes - List concern: _____ ☐ No _____

Anxiety:

1. Do you consider yourself an anxious person? If yes, list things that make you feel anxious:
   ☐ Yes - List: _____ ☐ No _____

Depression:

1. Do you feel depressed or down? If yes, list why you may feel this way or what makes you depressed:
   ☐ Yes - List: _____ ☐ No _____

Substance Abuse - Alcohol and Drugs:

1. Do either you, a friend, or a family member abuse alcohol and drugs?
   ☐ Yes - List: _____ ☐ No _____

Self-Harm:

1. Have you ever wanted to hurt yourself?
   ☐ Yes - List how you would hurt yourself: _____ ☐ No _____

WHAT'S YOUR GAME PLAN? • RELATIONSHIPS

Bullying/Cyberbullying:

1. Have you ever been bullied or been the recipient of cyberbullying?
   ☐ Yes - List situation: _____ ☐ No _____

Family or Guardian:

1. How would you rate your relationship with your family or guardian?
   ☐ Good ☐ Average ☐ Bad - List situation: _____

Friendship:

1. Are you in a peer-pressuring and/or non-supportive friend group?
   ☐ Yes - List your friends: _____ ☐ No _____

Peer Pressure:

1. Have you ever been put in a peer pressure situation?
   ☐ Yes - List situation: _____ ☐ No _____

List Your Stress Level Today (1 = not very stressed and 10 = very stressed) **(1-10)** _____

© 2023 Reflections Publishing LLC. All rights reserved.
This book is sold with the understanding that the publisher and the author are not engaged in rendering medical, legal, or other professional advice or services.
If professional assistance is required, the services of a competent professional should be sought.

The following are included in
The Resilience Game Plan: Student Edition

- **Section Twelve: 4114U • Notes**   **See Page 155**

- **Section Thirteen: 4114U • Glossary of Terms**   **See Page 169**

- **Section Fourteen: 4114U • Resources**   **See Page 171**

- **Create-Your-Own Life Topic**   **See Page 188-193**

- **Space to Download and Process Your Thoughts**   **See Page 194**

- ***The Resilience Game Plan* Certificate of Completion**   **See Page 195**

*Student Edition Pages

Section Eleven

4114U Appendix

(Page 151 in *The RGP: Student Edition*)

- Depression Game Plan - 102, 152
- Nutrition Game Plan - 103, 153
- Sample Competency-Based Grading Operating Procedures - 104-105
- Brain Power Color Chart - 106, 154
- *The Resilience Game Plan* Evidence-Base Intervention Program - 107

***Student Edition Pages**

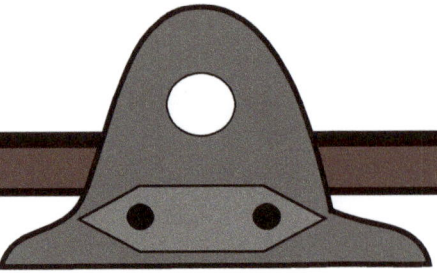

• Depression Game Plan •

Many people are struggling and not feeling like they did before the pandemic occurred. For some individuals, puberty triggers new feelings including depression, so be kind to yourself during these years. There are many ways to help you start feeling better, but know that people cannot read your mind; you need to communicate how you are feeling. **If you are in a downward spiral or experiencing an emergency, seek help immediately from a parent/guardian, school counselor, or medical professional.**

- Here is a checklist of things to discuss with your parent/guardian or medical professional:

☐ It is normal to experience a "Natural Depression"—where you may not feel like yourself for up to one year after a loved one has passed away. Share any losses, major changes, or trauma with your doctor that might affect how you feel.

☐ Sometimes your gut microbiome and the gut-brain axis can get out of sync, so have your doctor do a test for 16S rRNA gene sequencing. Also, try eating a Mediterranean diet which is known to help get your gut healthy.

☐ Ask your doctor to conduct a Pharmacogenetic (PGx) (Genomind™) or Psychotropic (GeneSight®) test to assess your genetics to create your personal therapeutic game plan. These tests identify potential gene-drug interactions and how your body metabolizes medicine.

☐ Ask your doctor to order an MTHFR blood test as this gene is often linked to depression.

☐ Check into Cognitive Behavior Therapy (CBT) or iCBT, as it is known to help treat depression.

☐ Pet therapy is notorious for assisting individuals who are depressed or suffering from post traumatic stress.

☐ Go outside, get grounded, and exercise every day—it is the best known therapy for depression.

☐ Socialize and find those 24/7 friends to reduce depression.

Just remember that doctors and educators went into their area of practice because they love to work with and help adolescents, so do not hesitate to talk to them and ask for assistance—whether medically or academically.

© 2024 Reflections Publishing LLC. All rights reserved.
This book is sold with the understanding that the publisher and the author are not engaged in rendering medical, legal, or other professional advice or services. If professional assistance is required, the services of a competent professional should be sought.

Date:

• Nutrition Game Plan •

Time:	Place:	Thoughts/Feelings:	Food:	# of Healthy Meals or Daily Calories:
Breakfast:				
Snack:				
Lunch:				
Snack:				
Dinner:				
Snack:				
Hydration:	I drank _____ 8oz glasses of water.			

© 2024 Reflections Publishing LLC. All rights reserved.

NUTRITION GAME PLAN

Sample Competency-Based Grading Operating Procedures

Percent	Letter Grade	Number Scale
90-100	A	4
80-89	B	3
70-79	C	2
50-69	IP	1

Student's Next Steps Competency-Based Grading Guide

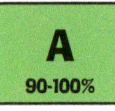

Exceeds Competency:
Student is ready for more challenging work

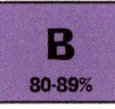

Meets Competency:
Student understands the majority, but needs more practice

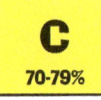

Minimum Competency:
Student is still learning, showing growth, and has reached minimum competency, but there is much more room for growth. (Students who are behind in school by more than one year must make MORE THAN a single year's growth in that competency as measured by the Chosen District Assessment in Math, Science, and/or English, or OTHER.)

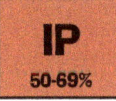

In Progress Competency:
Student has a lot of learning to do; student understands they have an opportunity to grow and make enormous progress. The teacher should work with the student to create an individualized learning plan to move to competency.
Note: Students do not receive a grade less than 50%. This is in line with the decimal scale for grades A-IP:
A: 90-100%
B: 80-89%
C: 70-79%
IP: 50-69% (The lowest score a student can receive is 50%.)

• Sample Competency-Based Grading Operating Procedures •

Competency-Based Grading:

In competency-based models, students advance upon mastery when they are ready, not based on an arbitrary academic calendar. Most importantly, students receive the timely, differentiated support they need in order to experience success and advance to the next level. Optimally, competencies are broad enough that student pathways and demonstrations of proficiency can be vastly different, organized to encourage and nurture student passions and questions. Failure is no longer an acceptable label for children or a feature of the system: if a student isn't proficient at a particular moment, then more learning and practice opportunities will be encouraged and facilitated. When proficiency is reached, the student will move on. The school bends to the child's learning needs, not the other way around.

Competencies are organized around specific learning outcomes that have meaning and importance in the world. For example, a competency might be defined as the ability to communicate with clarity and purpose, construct an evidence-based argument, or collaborate with others. In this sense, competencies tend to encompass an interrelated set of skills, knowledge, aptitudes, and/or capacities. In practice, competencies are often constructed as groupings of related skills or attributes that are purposefully designed to be explicit, measurable, transferable, and empowering to students (Sturgis, 2016).

Grading for Competency/Mastery

Each district/department's subject leaders determine the knowledge and set of skills needed for students to demonstrate mastery at each level. Those competencies will be clearly stated and used for pre- and post-assessments to determine where educators should focus their instruction and how to differentiate learning for individual students.

Reaching competency at each level within the given content area will be clearly delineated by district/department subject leaders asking the following questions at each level:

1. What does it mean to demonstrate competency in this course?
2. What are the competencies necessary to get there?
3. How do we frame assessments so students can demonstrate their learning?

Sample Competency-Based Grading Operating Procedures

Learning needs to be at the center of competency-based grading with scholars "not there yet" asking the common question, What do I still need to learn to demonstrate competency? As a result, schools will move from assignment-based to process-based—which is the process of learning.

Alternative Assessments

Because there is more than one way to demonstrate competency, schools should consider alternative assessments, even those created by students.

• Brain Power Color Chart •

Red – Amygdala
Processes emotions and certain types of learning and memory (Bear, Connors, & Paradiso, 2007).

Red Orange – Posterior Superior Temporal Sulcus
Plays a "role in detecting, predicting, and reasoning about social actions and the intentions underlying actions" (Allison et al., 2000).

Orange – Anterior Cingulate Cortex
"Complex cognitive functions, such as empathy, impulse control, emotion, and decision-making" (Neuroscientifically Challenged, 2023).

Peach – Nucleus Accumbens
Believed to "play an important role in motivation, reward, and addiction" (Neuroscientifically Challenged, 2023).

Pink – Dorsal Anterior Cingulate Cortex
Known for conflict monitoring, error processing, accomplishing tasks, and reaching goals (Encyclopedia of Neuroscience, 2009).

Magenta – Ventromedial Prefrontal Cortex
May reflect heightened sensitivity to threats and safety conditions (Britton et al., 2013).

Purple – Medial Prefrontal Cortex
Long-term assessments of your environmental experiences are stored here (Bonnici et al., 2012).

Light Purple – Ventral Striatum
Believed "to be involved in reward processing" (Neuroscientifically Challenged, 2023).

Blue – Hypothalamus
Processes your body temperature, ability to sleep, and need to eat and drink (Bear, Connors, & Paradiso, 2007).

Sky Blue – Insula
Believed "to play a role in a number of functions: self-awareness, perception, and cognition" (Neuroscientifically Challenged, 2023).

Light Blue – Temporo-Parietal Junction
"Involved specifically in reasoning about the contents of another person's mind"—theory of mind (Saxe & Kanwisher 2003).

Aqua – Lateral Occipital Cortex
"Known to be involved in visual object perception" (i.e., face-processing) (Nagy, Greenlee, & Kovács, 2012).

Golden Yellow – Cerebellum
"Role in memory, cognition, emotion, coordination, balance, posture, & smooth motor movements" (Neuroscientifically Challenged, 2023).

Yellow – Dorsolateral Prefrontal Cortex
Plays a role in impulse control (Bonnici et al., 2012).

Yellow Green – Medial Parienta
Plays a role in "memory recall, visual scene processing, navigation, and default mode network (Silson et al., 2019).

Green – Posterior Cingulate Cortex
Internally-generated thought processes and self-directed cognitions (Leech & Sharp, 2014).

Jade Green – Precuneus
Believed involvement "ranging from memory to consciousness" (Neuroscientifically Challenged, 2023).

Navy Blue – Thalamus
"Plays important roles in consciousness and arousal" (Neuroscientifically Challenged, 2023).

Burgandy – Superior Temporal Cortex
"Hub for social and cognition perception of faces..others' actions, mental states, and language" (Deen et al., 2015).

Brown – Orbitalfrontal Cortex
Believed "to be involved in decision-making and emotional processing" (Neuroscientifically Challenged, 2023).

Light Brown – Occipital Cortex
"Retinotopic organization of spatial frequency processing (Sasaki et al., 2001).

Tan – Putamen
Involved in motor control (Bear, Connors, & Paradiso, 2007).

Gray – Hippocampus
Plays a role in learning (Bear, Connors, & Paradiso, 2007); short-term memories are embedded here (Bonnici et al., 2012).

Black – Sugenual Cingulate
"Critical brain region in emotion processing and the pathogenesis of mood disorders" (Mayberg et al., 2005).

The Resilience Game Plan
Evidence-Based Intervention Program

Module 1: Introduction and Taking Pre-Assessments
Learning Theory: Pedagogical Strategies Retrieval Practice/Examination

↓

Module 2: Building Resilience with a Growth Mindset
Learning Theory: Growth Mindset Theory

↓

Module 3: Developing Global Changemakers
Learning Theory: Social Cognitive Theory

↓

Module 4: Creating a Personalized Game Plan for each Life Topic

- **Module 4.1: 4114U and Activity**
  Experiential Learning Theory

  →

- **Module 4.2: Understanding Brain Power**
  Learning Theory: Pedagogical Strategy Interleave Instruction

  →

- **Module 4.3: Learning Cognitive Skills**
  - Step 1: Expressive Writing
    Self-Affirmation Theory
    Spaced Instruction
  - Step 2: Gauging Feelings
    Learning Theory: Pedagogical Strategy Spaced Instruction
  - Step 3: Overcoming Obstacles
    Learning Theory: Pedagogical Strategy Spaced Instruction

  →

- **Module 4.4: Learning Communication Skills**
  Learning Theory: Pedagogical Strategy Variability of Learning Contexts

  →

- **Module 4.5: Learning Mindfulness Skills**
  Learning Theory: Pedagogical Strategy Interleave Instruction

↓

Module 5: Making New Habits Automatic
Learning Theory: Self-Regulation Theory

↓

Module 6: Setting Goals and Reducing Anxiety
Socio-Culturual Learning Theory: Internalization of Verbal Guidance

↓

Module 7: Conclusion and Taking Post-Assessments
Learning Theory: Pedagogical Strategies Retrieval Practice/Examination

Section Fifteen

4114U Supplemental References

(Supplemental Reference list to
The Resilience Game Plan: Student Edition's
Section Fifteen: 4114U - References
found on page 175.)

*Student Edition Pages

• 4114U Supplemental References •
(Supplemental Reference list to *The RGP: Student Edition's* Section Fourteen: 4114U References found on page 171.)

Allison, T., Puce, A., McCarthy, G. (2000). Social perception from visual cues: Role of the STS region. *Trends in Cognitive Sciences, 4*(7), 267–278. DOI: 10.1016/s1364-6613(00)01501-1

Anderson, M., Werner-Seidler, A., King, C., Gayed, A., Harvey, S. B., & O'Dea, B. (2019). Mental health training programs for secondary school teachers: A systematic review. *School Mental Health, 11*(3), 489–508.

Bandura, A. (2004). Health promotion by social cognitive means. *Health Education & Behavior, 31*, 143–164. DOI: 10.1177/1090198104263660

Baumeister, R. F., & Heatherton, T. F. (1996). Self-regulation failure: An overview. *An International Journal for the Advancement of Psychological Theory, 7*(1), 1–15. https://doi.org/10.1207/s15327965pli0701_1

Bear, M. F., Connors, B. W., & Paradiso, M. A. (2007). *Neuroscience: Exploring the brain*. Lippincott Williams & Wilkins.

Behan. (2020). The benefits of meditation and mindfulness practices during times of crisis such as COVID-19. *Irish Journal of Psychological Medicine, 37*(4), 256–258. https://doi.org/10.1017/ipm.2020.38

Bitsko, R. H., Claussen, A. H., Lichstein, J., Black, L. I., Jones, S. E., Danielson, M. L., Hoenig, J. M., Davis, J., Shane, P., Brody, D. J., Gyawali, S., M, M. J., Warner, M., Holland, K. M., Perou, R., Crosby, A. E., Blumberg, S. J., Avenevoli, S., Kaminski, J. W., Ghandour, R. M. (2022) Mental health surveillance among children—United States, 2013–2019. *CDC: Morbidity and Mortality Weekly Report Suppl 2022, 71*(Suppl. 2), 1–42. http://dx.doi.org/10.15585/mmwr.su7102a1

Bjork E. L. & Bjork R. A. (2011). *Making things hard on yourself, but in a good way: Creating desirable difficulties to enhance learning. In: Psychology and the real world: Essays illustrating fundamental contributions to society*. Worth Publishers.

Bueno-Notivol, J., Gracia-García, P., Olaya, B., Lasheras, I., López-Antón, R., & Santabárbara, J. (2021). Prevalence of depression during the COVID-19 outbreak: A meta-analysis of community-based studies. *International Journal of Clinical and Health Psychology, 21*(1), 100196–11. https://doi.org/10.1016/j.ijchp.2020.07.007

Carey, T. (2015). *Taming the tiger parent: How to put your child's well-being first in a competitive world*. Little Brown Book Group.

Chandra, A., & Minkovitz, C. S. (2006). Stigma starts early: Gender differences in teen willingness to use mental health services. *Journal of Adolescent Health, 38*(6), 754.e1–754.e8. https://doi.org/10.1016/j.jadohealth.2005.08.011

Department of Health, & NHS England. (2015). *Future in mind: promoting, protecting and improving our children and young people's mental health and wellbeing*.

Churcher, K., Downs, E., & Tewksbury, D. (2014). "Friending" Vygotsky: A social constructivist pedagogy of knowledge building through classroom social media use. *The Journal of Effective Teaching, 14*(1), 33–50.

Cole, J., Costafreda, S. G., McGuffin, P., & Fu, C. H. (2011). Hippocampal atrophy in first episode depression: A meta-analysis of magnetic resonance imaging studies. *Journal of Affective Disorders, 134*(1), 483–487. https://doi.org/10.1016/j.jad.2011.05.057

Cole, M. (1986). *The zone of proximal development: where culture and cognition create each other. In Wertsch, J. (Org.). Culture, Communication and Cognition: Vygotskian Perspective*. 146–161. Cambridge University Press.

Cowles, M., & Miller, A. (2009). Stress, cytokines and depressive illness. *Encyclopedia of Neuroscience*, 519–527. https://doi.org/10.1016/B978-008045046-9.00090-5

Day, L., Blades, R., Spence, C., & Ronicle, J. (2017). Mental health services and schools link pilots: Evaluation report. https://assets.publishing.service.gov.uk/government/uploads/system/uploads/attachment_data/file/590242/Evaluation_of_the_MH_services_and_schools_link_pilots-RR.pdf

Deen, B., Koldewyn, K., Kanwisher, N., Saxe, R. (2015) Functional organization of social perception and cognition in the superior temporal sulcus, *Cerebral Cortex, 25*(1), 4596–4609. https://doi.org/10.1093/cercor/bhv111

Department of Health, & Department for Education. (2017). *Transforming children and young people's mental health provision: a green paper*. APS Group.

Dirksen, J. (2016). *Design for how people learn (1st edition)*. New Riders.

Eklund, K., & Dowdy, E. (2014). Screening for behavioral and emotional risk versus traditional school identification methods. *School Mental Health, 6*, 40–49.

Evans, R., Russell, A. E., Mathews, F., Parker, R., & Janssens, A. (2017). Report: GW4 children and young people's self-harm and suicide research collaboration, *Children & Young People Now, 2017*(2), 1–106. https://doi.org/10.12968/cypn.2017.2.35

Evans, R., & Hurrell, C. (2016). The role of schools in children and young people's self-harm and suicide: systematic review and meta-ethnography of qualitative research. *BMC Public Health, 16*(401), 1–16. https://doi.org/10.1186/s12889-016-3065-2

Fazel, M., Hoagwood, K., Stephan, S., & Ford, T. (2014). Mental health interventions in school in high-income countries. *The Lancet Psychiatry, 1*, 377–387. https://doi.org/10.1016/S2215-0366(14) 70312-8.

Good, C., Rattan, A., & Dweck, C. S. (2012). Why do women opt out? Sense of belonging and women's representation in mathematics. *Journal of Personality and Social Psychology, 102*, 700–717. https://doi.org/10.1037/a0026659

Gordon, J. S., Sbarra, D., Armin, J., Pace, T. W. W., Gniady, C., & Barraza, Y. (2021). Use of a guided imagery mobile app (see me serene) to reduce COVID-19–related stress: Pilot feasibility study. *JMIR Formative Research, 5*(10), e32353–e32353. https://doi.org/10.2196/32353

Gratzer, D. & Khalid-Khan, F. (2016). Internet-delivered cognitive behavioural therapy in the treatment of psychiatric illness. *Canadian Medical Association Journal (CMAJ), 188*(4), 263–272. https://doi.org/10.1503/cmaj.150007

Green, J. G., Oblath, R., & Holt, M. (2022). Teacher and school characteristics associated with the identification and referral of adolescent depression and oppositional defiant disorders by U.S. teachers. *School Mental Health, 14*(3), 498–513. https://doi.org/10.1007/s12310-021-09491-1

Greenberg, P. E., Fournier, A.-A., Sisitsky, T., Pike, C. T., & Kessler, R. C. (2015). The economic burden of adults with major depressive disorder in the United States (2005 and 2010). *Journal Clinical Psychiatry 76*, 155–162. https://doi.10.4088/JCP.14m09298

Guthold, R., Newby, H., Keogh, S., Afifi, R. A., Austrian, K., Baird, S., Blum, R. W., Bundy, D. A. P., Deardorff, J., Engel, D., Klein, J. D., Kostelecky, S. M., Mackworth-Young, C., Marquez, J., NicGabhainn, S., Requejo, J., Ross, D. A., Saewyc, E., & Mohan, A. (2023). Developing a global approach for measurement of adolescent well-being. *Journal of Adolescent Health, 73*(6), 972–974. https://doi.org/10.1016/j.jadohealth.2023.08.029

Heatherton, T. F. (2010). Neuroscience of self and self-regulation. *Annual review of psychology, 62*, 363. https://doi.org/10.1146/annurev.psych.121208.131616

Humphrey, N., & Wigelsworth, M. (2016). Making the case for universal school-based mental health screening. *Emotional and Behavioural Difficulties, 21*, 22–42. https://doi.org/10.1080/13632752.2015.1120051

İrengün, O., & Arıkboğa, Ş. (2015). The effect of personality traits on social entrepreneurship intentions: A field research. *Procedia, Social and Behavioral Sciences, 195*, 1186–1195. https://doi.org/10.1016/j.sbspro.2015.06.172

John-Steiner, V. & Mahn, H. (1996). Sociocultural approaches to learning and development: A Vygotskian framework. *Educational Psychologist, 31*(3-4), 191–206. https://doi.org/10.1207/s15326985ep3103&4_4

Jokela, M., Ferrie, J., & Kivimäki, M. (2009). Childhood problem behaviors and death by midlife: The British national child development study. *Journal of the American Academy of Child & Adolescent Psychiatry, 48*, 19–24.

Kolb, D. A. (1984). *Experiential learning: Experience as the source of learning and development*. Prentice-Hall.

Li, W., Mao, Y., & Hu, B. (2022). Will exposure to different consequences of prosocial behavior always lead to subsequent prosocial behavior among adolescents: An experimental study of short videos. *Frontiers in Psychology, 13*, 927952. https://doi.org/10.3389/fpsyg.2022.927952

Mater, N., Daher, W., & Mahamid, F. (2023). The effect of STEAM activities based on experiential learning on ninth graders' mental motivation. *European Journal of Investigation in Health, Psychology and Education, 13*(7), 1229–1244. https://doi.org/10.3390/ejihpe13070091

Mayberg, H. S., Lozano, A. M., Voon, V., McNeely, H. E., Seminowicz, D., Hamani, C., Schwalb, J. M., Kennedy, S. H. (2005). Deep brain stimulation for treatment-resistant depression. *Neuron, 45*, 651–660. https://doi.org/10.1016/j.neuron.2005.02.014

McAdams, C. J., & Krawczyk, D. C. (2014). Who am I? How do I look? Neural differences in self-identity in anorexia nervosa. *Social Cognitive and Affective Neuroscience, 9*(1), 12–21. https://doi.org/10.1093/scan/nss093

Miller, P. (2016). *Theories of developmental psychology* (6th ed.). Worth Publishers.

Nagy, K., Greenlee, M. W., & Kovács, G. (2012). The lateral occipital cortex in the face perception network: An effective connectivity study. *Frontiers in Psychology, 3*, 23246. https://doi.org/10.3389/fpsyg.2012.00141

National Health Service England. (2016). *The five year forward view for mental health: A report from the independent Mental Health Taskforce to the NHS in England*. (NHS England, Ed.)..

Nordh, M., Wahlund, T., Jolstedt, M., Sahlin, H., Bjureberg, J., Ahlen, J., Lalouni, M., Salomonsson, S., Vigerland, S., Lavner, M., Öst, L.-G., Lenhard, F., Hesser, H., Mataix-Cols, D., Högström, J., & Serlachius, E. (2021). Therapist-guided internet-delivered cognitive behavioral therapy vs internet-delivered supportive therapy for children and adolescents with social anxiety disorder: A randomized clinical trial. *Archives of General Psychiatry, 78*(7), 705–713. https://doi.org/10.1001/jamapsychiatry.2021.0469

Nouretdinov, I., Costafreda, S. G., Gammerman, A., Chervonenkis, A., Vovk, V., Vapnik, V., & Fu, C. H. (2011). Machine learning classification with confidence: Application of transductive conformal predictors to MRI-based diagnostic and prognostic markers in depression. *NeuroImage, 56*(2), 809–813. https://doi.org/10.1016/j.neuroimage.2010.05.023

Patel, V., Flisher, A. J., Hetrick, S., & McGorry, P. (2007). Mental health of young people: a global public-health challenge. *Lancet, 369*, 1302–1313. https://doi.org/10.1016/S0140-6736(07)60368-7.

Pennebaker, J. W. (2018). Expressive writing in psychological science. *Perspectives on Psychological Science, 13*(2), 226–229. https://doi.org/10.1177/1745691617707315

Rao, U., & Chen, L. A. (2009). Characteristics, correlates, and outcomes of childhood and adolescent depressive disorders. *Dialogues in Clinical Neuroscience 11*, 45–62. https://doi.org/10.31887/DCNS.2009.11.1/urao

Rohrer D., Dedrick R. F., & Burgess K. (2014) The benefit of interleaved mathematics practice is not limited to superficially similar kinds of problems. *Psychonomic Bulletin & Review, 21*(5), 1323–1330. https://doi.org/10.3758/s13423-014-0588-3

Rosenburg, B. M., Kodish, T., Cohen, Z. D., Gong-Guy, E., & Craske, M. G. (2022). A novel peer-to-peer coaching program to support digital mental health: Design and implementation. *JMIR Mental Health, 9*(1), e32430–e32430. https://doi.org/10.2196/32430

Sasaki, Y., Hadjikhani, N., Fischl B., Liu, A. K., Marret, S., Dale, A. M., Tootell, R. B. H. (2001) Local and global attention are mapped retinotopically in human occipital cortex. *Proceedings of the National Academy of Sciences, 98*(4) 2077-2082. https://doi.org/10.1073/pnas.98.4.2077

Scher, C. D., Forde, D. R., McQuaid, J. R., & Stein, M. B. (2004). Prevalence and demographic correlates of childhood maltreatment in an adult community sample. *Child Abuse & Neglect, 28*(2), 167–180. https://doi.org/10.1016/j.chiabu.2003.09.012

Schmidt R. A., & Bjork R. A. (2017). New conceptualizations of practice: Common principles in three paradigms suggest new concepts for training. *Psychological Science, 3*(4), 207–218. https://doi.org/10.1111/j.1467-9280.1992.tb00029.x

Selemon, L. D., & Zecevic, N. (2015). Schizophrenia: A tale of two critical periods for prefrontal cortical development. *Translational Psychiatry, 5*(8), e623–e623. https://doi.org/10.1038/tp.2015.115

Shah, J. Y. (2005). The automatic pursuit and management of goals. *Current Directions Psychological Science, 14*(1), 10–13. https://doi.org/10.1111/j.0963-7214.2005.00325

Shvarts, A., & Bakker, A. (2019). The early history of the scaffolding metaphor: Bernstein, Luria, Vygotsky, and before. *Mind, Culture, and Activity, 26*(1), 4–23. https://doi.org/10.1080/10749039.2019.1574306

Silson, E. H., Steel, A., Kidder, A., Gilmore, A. W., Baker, C. I. (2019). Distinct subdivisions of human medial parietal cortex support recollection of people and places. *eLife 8*. e47391. https://doi.org/10.7554/eLife.47391

Smith, S. M. (1984). A comparison of two techniques for reducing context-dependent forgetting. *Memory & Cognition, 12*(5), 477–482. https://doi.org/10.3758/BF03198309

Smolucha, L., & Smolucha, F. (2021). Vygotsky's theory in-play: early childhood education. *Early Child Development and Care, 191*(7-8), 1041–1055. https://doi.org/10.1080/03004430.2020.1843451

Soneson, E., Howarth, E., Ford, T., Humphrey, A., Jones, P. B., Thompson Coon, J., Rogers, M., & Anderson, J. K. (2020). Feasibility of school-based identification of children and adolescents experiencing, or at-risk of developing, mental health difficulties: A systematic review. *Prevention Science: The official journal of the Society for Prevention Research, 21*(5), 581–603. https://doi.org/10.1007/s11121-020-01095-6

Stanley, B., & Brown, G. K. (2012). Safety planning intervention: A brief intervention to mitigate suicide risk. *Cognitive and Behavioral Practice, 19*(2), 256-264. DOI: 10.1016/j.cbpra.2011.01.001

Sweller, J. (1988), Cognitive load during problem solving: Effects on learning. *Cognitive Science, 12*, 257-285. https://doi.org/10.1207/s15516709cog1202_4

Teicher, M. H., & Samson, J. A. (2016). Annual research review: Enduring neurobiological effects of childhood abuse and neglect. *Journal of Child Psychology and Psychiatry, 57*(3), 241–266. https://doi.org/10.1111/jcpp.12507

Tymofiyeva, O., Zhou, V. X., Lee, C.-M., Xu, D., Hess, C. P., & Yang, T. T. (2020). MRI insights into adolescent neurocircuitry–A vision for the future. *Frontiers in Human Neuroscience, 14*(237), 1-27. https://doi.org/10.3389/fnhum.2020.00237

United States Preventive Services Task Force. (2022). Screening for depression and suicide risk in children and adolescents: U.S. Preventive Services Task Force recommendation statement. *JAMA, 328*(15), 1534–1542. DOI: 10.1001/jama.2022.16946

Vigo, D., Thornicroft, G., & Atun, R. (2016). Estimating the true global burden of mental illness. *The Lancet. Psychiatry, 3*(2), 171–178. https://doi.org/10.1016/S2215-0366(15)00505-2

Wester, K. L., Wachter Morris, C., & Williams, B. (2018). Nonsuicidal self-injury in the schools: A tiered prevention approach for reducing social contagion. *Professional School Counseling, 21*(1), 1096-2409. https://doi.org/10.5330/1096-2409-21.1.142

Winsler, A., Fernyhough, C., & Montero, I. (2009). *Private speech, executive functioning, and the development of self-regulation.* Cambridge: Cambridge University Press.

Wong, J. M. W., Ebbeling, C. B., Robinson, L., Feldman, H. A., & Ludwig, D. S. (2017). Effects of advice to drink 8 cups of water per day in adolescents with overweight or obesity: A randomized clinical trial. *JAMA Pediatrics, 171*(5), e170012. https://doi.org/10.1001/jamapediatrics.2017.0012

Yeager, D. S., & Dweck, C. S. (2012). Mindsets that promote resilience: When students believe that personal characteristics can be developed. *Educational Psychologist, 47,* 302– 314. https://doi.org/10.1080/00461520.2012.722805

Zavaruieva, I., Bondarenko, L., & Fedko, O. (2022). The role of colour coding of educational materials when studying grammatical categories of the Ukrainian language by foreign students. *Review of Education, 10,* e3312. https://doi.org/10.1002/rev3.3312

www.ingramcontent.com/pod-product-compliance
Lightning Source LLC
Chambersburg PA
CBHW061749290426
44108CB00028B/2935